AF572023

LIVING WITH THE SCRIPTURES

VOLUME 1

Satsvarūpa dāsa Goswami

GĪTĀ-NĀGARĪ PRESS
Philadelphia

Printed in the United States of America
Limited Edition: 3,000 copies

Library of Congress Cataloging in Publication Data

Gosvāmī, Satsvarūpa Dāsa 1939 –
Living With The Scriptures
1. International Society for Krishna Consciousness
2. Religious life (Hinduism) 1. Title.

BL1285.84.G66 1984 294.5'92 84-21238
ISBN: 0-911233-26-1 (v. 1)

Table of Contents

His Divine Grace
A. C. Bhaktivedanta Swami Prabhupāda
Founder-*Ācārya* of the International Society for Krishna Consciousness

Preface

This is a book of essays based on selected verses of Vedic literature. I have chosen verses that have special meaning in my life, with the hope that discussing them will make for interesting and instructive reading.

In the life of His Divine Grace A. C. Bhaktivedanta Swami Prabhupāda, there also appeared to be particular verses which especially guided him. For example, there is the following *śloka* from the *Śrīmad-Bhāgavatam:*

> *yasyāham anugṛhṇāmi*
> *hariṣye tad-dhanaṁ śanaiḥ*
> *tato 'dhanaṁ tyajanty asya*
> *sva-janā duḥkha-duḥkhitam*

> When I feel especially mercifully disposed towards someone, I gradually take away all his material possessions. His friends and relatives then reject this poverty-stricken and most wretched fellow.

When Śrīla Prabhupāda was attempting to develop his business and family and yet found frustration in these affairs, this verse from the *Bhāgavatam* was particularly applicable to him, and he could find solace and joy in it.

Sometimes life in the material world forces us to see the truth of particular verses and purports, such as the *yasyāham* verse as it was revealed to Śrīla Prabhupāda. And sometimes our spiritual master recommends a particular verse for us, just as Īśvara Purī recommended the *harer nāma* verse to Lord Caitanya Mahāprabhu. Or sometimes one keeps meeting certain verses like special, providential friends and guides.

The meaning of a certain verse may elude one for years and disturb or follow one in an unanswered way, until gradually Kṛṣṇa reveals Himself to His sincere devotee. Śrīla Prabhupāda informs us how, after years of consideration, a certain verse spoken by Prahlāda Mahārāja came to him as a solution to a dilemma. The dilemma occurred when Śrīla Prabhupāda saw his spiritual master order a snake to be killed. Śrīla Prabhupāda said he had a kind of doubt or puzzlement about why a *sādhu,* who is always nonviolent, would order the snake to be killed. Years later, Prabhupāda encountered a verse by Prahlāda Mahārāja in which Prahlāda states, *modeta sādhur api vṛścika-sarpa-hatyā* (*Bhag.* 7.9.14), that even a *sādhu* is glad when a snake or snakelike demon such as Hiraṇyakaśipu is killed. Prabhupāda felt much relieved, and his understanding was clear about his Guru Mahārāja's action.

Special attention was given by Śrīla Prabhupāda's spiritual master, Śrīla Bhaktisiddhānta Sarasvatī Ṭhākura, to the very first verse of the *Śrīmad-Bhāgavatam, janmādy asya yataḥ.* Śrīla Bhaktisiddhānta lectured on this verse daily for three straight months. Prabhupāda also informs us that Śrīla Viśvanātha Cakravartī Ṭhākura's commentary to *Bhagavad-gītā* 2.41 played a very important part in the life of Śrīla Prabhupāda.

Śrīla Viśvanātha Cakravartī emphasizes that the order of the spiritual master is as important to the disciple as the life air is to the living body. Only after reading this verse and commentary did Bhaktivinoda Ṭhākura fully realize the import of the *guru*-disciple relationship.

Lord Caitanya placed special importance on the *ātmārāma* verse of the *Śrīmad-Bhāgavatam:*

ātmārāmāś ca munayo
nirgranthā apy urukrame
kurvanty ahaitukīṁ bhaktim
ittham-bhūta-guṇo hariḥ

> All different varieties of *ātmārāmas* [those who take pleasure in *ātmā*, or spirit self], especially those established on the path of self-realization, though freed from all kinds of material bondage, desire to render unalloyed devotional service unto the Personality of Godhead.This means that the Lord possesses transcendental qualities and therefore can attract everyone, including liberated souls.
>
> (*Bhāg*. 1.7.10)

Lord Caitanya explained this verse at great length on two occasions — once to Sārvabhauma Bhaṭṭācārya and again to Sanātana Gosvāmī, to whom Lord Caitanya explained the verse in sixty-one different ways.

Another highly valuable verse from the *Śrīmad-Bhāgavatam* was recited and appreciated by Mādhavendra Purī with intense ecstasy:

ayi dīna-dayārdra nātha he
mathurā-nātha kadāvalokyase
hṛdayaṁ tvad-aloka-kātaraṁ
dayita bhrāmyati kiṁ karomy aham

> O My Lord! O most merciful master! O master of Mathurā! When shall I see You again? Because of My not seeing You, My agitated heart has become unsteady. O most beloved one, what shall I do now?
>
> (Cc. *Mādhya* 4.197)

It is said that this verse was so rare that only three individuals in the whole world could understand it, namely Lord Caitanya, Mādhavendra Purī, and Śrīmatī Rādhārāṇī.

Certain verses composed by Rūpa Gosvāmī moved Lord Caitanya Mahāprabhu to ecstasy and caused transformations of His mind and body. And certain verses from the Tenth Canto caused Lord Caitanya to enter into trances of separation from Kṛṣṇa.

Although all of the verses of the *Śrīmad-Bhāgavatam* and *Bhagavad-gītā*, as well as other Vedic literatures, are absolute and nondifferent from Kṛṣṇa, individual devotees nevertheless associate with certain verses, find special meanings in them, and instruct them to their followers.

My own experience with the scriptures does not consist of accounts of great ecstasies or sudden, earth-shattering revelations. Nevertheless, by the grace of Śrīla Prabhupāda, I have been living with the scriptures for almost twenty years, and somehow certain particular verses and purports have remained with me as special guides.

My selection herein is personal. I have had particular experiences with these verses and wanted to share and explain them from an individual point of view.

Through this selection and discussion I hope to draw myself and my readers into the inconceivable, often elusive realm of *kṛṣṇa-kathā*. Sometimes we are moved by a particular verse or *līlā* of Kṛṣṇa, but when we go to share it with a friend, we find they are in a different mood or on a different "wave length" and are not able to really appreciate our individual realization. And sometimes when our friend comes to us with his Kṛṣṇa conscious realization, we may be distracted or otherwise absorbed. But when we read submissively, we are in a mood to more patiently give our time and share the wave length of another devotee. And when this patience is rightly reciprocated by the author, we may thus encounter the scriptures in a more enlivening and penetrating way and see new lights within them. As devotees, we live not only *by* the *śāstra* (in the sense that they govern us), but also *with* the *śāstra*, and we may grow with them just as we grow and serve in the personal association of *guru* and *sādhu*.

I
The Devotee Is a Preacher

prāyena deva munayaḥ sva-vimukti-kāmā
maunaṁ caranti vijane na parārtha-niṣṭhāḥ
naitān vihāya kṛpaṇān vimumukṣa eko
nānyaṁ tvad asya śaraṇaṁ bhramato 'nupaśye

"My dear Lord Nṛsiṁhadeva, I see that there are many saintly persons indeed, but they are interested only in their own deliverance. Not caring for the big cities and towns, they go to the Himalayas or the forest to meditate with vows of silence [*mauna-vrata*]. They are not interested in delivering others. As for me, however, I do not wish to be liberated alone, leaving aside all these poor fools and rascals. I know that without Kṛṣṇa consciousness, without taking shelter of Your lotus feet, one cannot be happy. Therefore I wish to bring them back to shelter at Your lotus feet."

(*Bhāg*. 7.9.44)

Whenever I feel my tendency for becoming reclusive growing too strong, this powerful Vaiṣṇava prayer reminds me of my higher obligation. I am not the only one with a tendency toward seclusion, but I will tell you my version of it.

A solitary tendency was always there in me, even before the time I met Śrīla Prabhupāda and became a devotee in Kṛṣṇa consciousness. But so was the drive to socialize and thus to lord it over others — a process which always brought hurt and frustration.

In my eclectic search for the truth, I sometimes encountered writings in which solitude was encouraged as a rare blessing; he who could be satisfied while alone was praised as wise. My reading of the poet Rilke seemed to confirm this, as did the teachings of Lao Tse and the Taoists.

Since I was living in New York City, there was no question of "solitary confinement" or hermitage. Yet the pleasures of solitude—a walk in the park alone, reading a book, writing, thinking or contemplating late into the night—these ranked higher to me than all comings-together. Or so I liked to think in my romance of solitude. How lonely I really was! Yet, inevitably, attempts for deep satisfaction in union with others left me finally seeking out a lonely place for the ultimate solace—the joy of being alone. Even my closer friends tended to be solitary types or persons who at least appreciated the philosophy of attaining peace by being contemplative, free, alone. One cultivated aloneness even in the midst of others. Like Herman Hesse's character Steppenwolf or Dostoevski's antihero of *Notes from the Underground,* one accepted as destiny being apart from the crowd.

I can now see that my attempts to appreciate and romanticize solitude were a kind of frustrated renunciation. I did not know there was any other way to avoid suffering except to lessen it by being alone, free from the major hurts caused by others.

Once, while an illness confined me to bed for a few weeks, I looked through many books, and my taste was spiritual. I read the Bible, Lao Tse, and paperback editions of *Bhagavad-gītā.* I was particularly attracted to the *Upaniṣads,* which spoke of an inner Self as the One Truth beyond all illusory shows of this temporary existence. I recall one passage:

> It is not for the sake of the husband, my beloved, that the husband is dear, but for the sake of the self. It is not for the sake of the wife, my beloved, that the wife is dear, but for the sake of

> the self. It is not for the sake of the children, my beloved, that the children are dear, but for the sake of the self. It is not for the sake of wealth, my beloved, that wealth is dear, but for the sake of the self. It is not for the sake of the *brāhmaṇas*, my beloved, that the *brāhmaṇas* are held in reverence, but for the sake of the self. It is not for the sake of the *kṣatriyas*, my beloved, that the *kṣatriyas* are held in honor, but for the sake of the self. It is not for the sake of the higher worlds, my beloved, that the higher worlds are desired, but for the sake of the self. It is not for the sake of the gods, my beloved, that the gods are worshiped, but for the sake of the self. It is not for the sake of the creatures, my beloved, that the creatures are prized, but for the sake of the self. It is not for the sake of itself, my beloved, that anything whatever is esteemed. The self, Maitreyi, is to be known. Hear about it, reflect upon it, meditate upon it. By knowing the self, my beloved, through hearing, reflections, and meditation, one comes to know all things.

This was inspiring and attractive to me. But how to truly contact the Self and live in truth?

From my reading, I came to feel that the peace and bliss of the *ātmā* was something to be obtained by an austere and contemplative life of solitude. Alone and bedridden, I would sometimes think that when I got well, I should enter a Franciscan monastery. I was, after all, raised as a Catholic. But what would I do about all of my material desires—desires to be loved and appreciated in the company of a beloved or friends? It would be a very stern, ascetic decision to reject life in favor of monastic meditation. And although I was somewhat serious about my spiritual and Eastern readings, I really did not think I could make it as a monk. And so I returned to my job and the world of social welfare work in New York City. And I returned to my usual, frustrating activities of moving back and forth between trying to enjoy and trying to renounce. Spirituality and solitude—which I thought went together—were to me a kind of unobtainable ideal.

When I first met Śrīla Prabhupāda, I thought he also must be teaching of reaching the *ātmā* by solitary meditation. Sure, we chanted *together,* but did not the *Bhagavad-gītā* (13.11) teach that knowledge meant "aspiring to live in a solitary place" and "detachment from the general mass of people"? Before too long I asked Śrīla Prabhupāda about the *Gītā's* verse concerning solitude. To my surprise, he explained that solitude means avoiding the nondevotee. To be with devotees was as good as being alone; in fact, it was much better. It was pure association, and it led us on to our personal relationship with Lord Kṛṣṇa. Because I had accepted Śrīla Prabhupāda as my spiritual master, I knew that he was right. But it would take me some time to realize this lesson.

Before long Śrīla Prabhupāda was liberating us from our many material and so-called spiritual misconceptions and speculations. Very soon he had us chanting in the parks and distributing *Back to Godheads* to the nondevotees. And I was happy to live in the company of his disciples.

Although this prayer by Prahlāda Mahārāja occurs in the Seventh Canto of the *Śrīmad-Bhāgavatam,* which was not published until 1976, Śrīla Prabhupāda had given it to us much earlier in talks and writings. I remember how the topic of Prahlāda Mahārāja's verse came up in 1966 in the storefront at 26 Second Avenue. Prabhupāda was lecturing that Kṛṣṇa consciousness relieves one of all material distress. When one attains Kṛṣṇa consciousness he becomes fully happy, without any anxiety. After the lecture, Kīrtanānanda asked Śrīla Prabhupāda whether there was such a thing as a spiritual unhappiness caused by the fact that a devotee could not convince others to become Kṛṣṇa conscious.

"Yes," Prabhupāda replied, and by his demeanor we could understand that he was pleased with the question. We could sense that a very meaningful point had been appreciated by Kīrtanānanda and that Prabhupāda wanted us all to grasp the conclusion. "Yes," Prabhupāda said, "that is the unhappiness of a Vaiṣṇava." Śrīla Prabhupāda then explained Prahlāda Mahārāja's prayer. Suddenly, by Kīrtanānanda's question and Śrīla Prabhupāda's answer, we had all gone a further stage in our spiritual consciousness. We had moved beyond the practice of spiritual life merely for the sake of oneself.

When the Seventh Canto was published, Śrīla Prabhupāda spelled it out more clearly, lest there be any doubt:

> The members of the Kṛṣṇa consciousness movement are not at all interested in so-called meditation in the Himalayas or the forest, where one will only make a show of meditation, nor are they interested in opening many schools for *yoga* and meditation in the cities. Rather, every member of the Kṛṣṇa consciousness movement is interested in going door to door to try to convince people about the teachings of *Bhagavad-gītā As It Is,* the teachings of Lord Caitanya. That is the purpose of the Hare Kṛṣṇa movement.

As I understand this verse and purport, to be an active preacher in the mood of Prahlāda Mahārāja one has to first be internally convinced and fixed in Kṛṣṇa consciousness. My previous seeking for a state of inner peace not dependent on the material world was not an entirely mistaken idea. But I had not known where to find that peace. It was all vague and took the form of a frustrated renunciation, with only a dim glimmer of spiritual hope. When one is aware of one's self as spirit soul, and when one understands the soul's eternal relationship with Kṛṣṇa, then only does well-being begin. Otherwise, everyone in the world is in anxiety, and everyone is terribly alone and isolated, regardless of how they try to cover it up. Whether a person appears to be very popular and dominating in the midst of social settings or whether he or she is a loner, everyone is factually alone. No other person or group can take an individual's *karma* and share it completely, and no one dies with us within our own consciousness when we die. No one appreciates exactly how nice we are, and no one knows the long history of our sorrow. Kṛṣṇa consciousness, therefore, not only provides association with spiritual persons, but it also gives the solution to loneliness. That solution is self-realization by understanding that Kṛṣṇa is one's best friend. Even from the beginning of taking to the process of *bhakti-yoga* this realization takes hold, and a devotee feels immense relief.

The internal peace and well-being that comes through Kṛṣṇa consciousness is an important quality for preachers who go out and meet the nondevotees. Śrīla Prabhupāda describes this quality of the renounced person in Kṛṣṇa consciousness:

> One must be fully convinced that Kṛṣṇa or the Supreme Personality of Godhead in His localized aspect as Paramātmā is always within, and that He is seeing everything and He always knows what one intends to do. One must thus have firm conviction that Kṛṣṇa as Paramātmā will take care of a soul surrendered to Him. "I shall never be alone," one should think. "Even if I live in the darkest regions of a forest I shall be accompanied by Kṛṣṇa, and He will give me all protection." That conviction is called *abhayam,* fearlessness. This state of mind is necessary for a person in the renounced order of life.
>
> (Bg. 16.3, purport)

I remember that soon after becoming Śrīla Prabhupāda's disciple, I felt new strength and confidence when mixing with people. The workers at the welfare office could also see that I had attained a kind of inner solidity, a peacefulness that could not be easily ruffled. Taking advantage of this, my supervisor once asked me if I would be willing to work for a notoriously difficult person, a Miss Robinson, who was the terror of the office for her insulting, emotional behavior. Miss Robinson would sometimes come to the office storming in rage over nothing apparent, and she would turn that rage on her co-workers at the slightest provocation. But because I had Śrīla Prabhupāda, Kṛṣṇa, the devotees, and the temple to live for, she did not bother me. As long as I was able to execute my service of earning money for Kṛṣṇa, I could not be reached by the petty disturbances around me.

But what about the preaching mood itself, the compassion to approach the nondevotee, to undergo trials and to work on Kṛṣṇa's behalf? That is the essence of this verse by Prahlāda Mahārāja, and Śrīla Prabhupāda explains how this attitude comes about. "Every member of the Kṛṣṇa consciousness movement is interested in going door to door to try to convince people about the teachings of *Bhagavad-gītā As It Is*," Śrīla Prabhupāda states in the purport to the verse. And for the best training in the life of the Vaiṣṇava, the "door to door" welfare work should begin early in one's Kṛṣṇa consciousness. It is by hearing as well as by actually going door to door that we gain conviction in the mission of the preacher. Other ideal forms of preaching include going out with a party of seasoned devotees to chant the Hare Kṛṣṇa *mantra* in a public place and to approach passersby with books or *Back to Godhead* magazines. A beginner can at least accompany the devotees who are doing this, watch them, and imbibe their dedication and blissfulness. Eventually, a devotee comes to understand that *any* work done on behalf of the spiritual master to further the aims of the Kṛṣṇa consciousness movement is all part of preaching the word of Kṛṣṇa consciousness and engaging conditioned souls in His eternal devotional service.

By associating with Śrīla Prabhupāda we soon imbibed his enthusiasm for preaching, and we would go out regularly to preach in the city. I remember hawking mimeographed *Back to Godheads* on Eighth Street and St. Mark's Place, loudly calling out to the passersby. When they would stop I would tell them about the essay by Allen Ginsberg or about some of the other articles in the magazine. With other devotees, I would sell BTG's in front of movie theaters before showtime. We would also regularly go out and chant publicly. Walking double-file along the sidewalks, playing hand cymbals and mṛdaṅga drums, and chanting Hare Kṛṣṇa, we would proceed from the Lower East Side to the West Village and then return. Tompkins Square Park was another good place to chant, especially on weekends, and sometimes Prabhupāda would come with us. After moving to Boston I would preach to college students in their dorms and hold as many lecture programs as I could.

Śrīla Prabhupāda quotes Prahlāda Mahārāja as saying, "I know that without Kṛṣṇa, without taking shelter of Your lotus feet, one cannot be happy." And Śrīla Prabhupāda declares, "the members of the Kṛṣṇa consciousness movement must be convinced that without Kṛṣṇa one cannot be happy." When one is able to see through the eyes of the scriptures how people are being entrapped in suffering due to their own material desires and their lack of Kṛṣṇa consciousness, and when one can understand that no one can escape from the suffering even after repeated births and deaths, then such a realized devotee steps forward to offer relief to the suffering. "Without Kṛṣṇa consciousness, they are all condemned," the preacher thinks, and so he goes from town to town with the message of Kṛṣṇa. He thinks, "I do not wish to go back to Godhead alone," and he prays to Kṛṣṇa, "Give me some strength so that I can deliver some of them. It is not possible to deliver all of them, but let me deliver some." When a devotee attains to this stage, then he is actually a Vaiṣṇava. Bhaktivinoda Ṭhākura has written that one can understand who is a Vaiṣṇava by considering how many conditioned souls he has brought to Kṛṣṇa. One may try for oneself only, and one may consider that one is very advanced, but such solitary spiritual life is not much appreciated by Kṛṣṇa. If, however, one approaches the conditioned souls and introduces them to Kṛṣṇa consciousness, that will very quickly catch the attention of Kṛṣṇa. Lord Kṛṣṇa declares in the *Bhagavad-gītā* that there will never be a servant more dear to Him than he who preaches to devotees or who helps people become devotees. The members of the Kṛṣṇa consciousness movement, the followers of Śrīla Prabhupāda, are in disciplic succession from Prahlāda Mahārāja, and we are duty-bound to follow his compassionate mood.

I have now come to realize that the spiritual ideal is not to be alone, but to preach. I still have my solitary tendencies, but Śrīla Prabhupāda's order to preach, as perfectly summed up in Prahlāda Mahārāja's verse, keeps me from indulging in solitude. Śrīla Prabhupāda has also mentioned this in a purport within the *Caitanya-caritāmṛta:*

> At the present moment we see that some members of the International Society for Krishna Consciousness are tending to leave their preaching activities in order to sit in a solitary place. This is not a very good sign. It is a fact that Śrīla Bhaktisiddhānta Sarasvatī Ṭhākura has condemned this process for neophytes. He has even stated in a song, *pratiṣṭhāra tare, nirjanera ghare, tava hari-nāma kevala kaitava.* Sitting in a solitary place intending to chant the Hare Kṛṣṇa *mahā-mantra* is considered a cheating process. This practice is not possible for neophytes at all. The neophyte devotee must act and work very laboriously under the direction of the spiritual master, and he must thus preach the cult of Śrī Caitanya Mahāprabhu. Only after maturing in devotion can he sit down in a solitary place to chant the Hare Kṛṣṇa *mahā-mantra* as Śrī Caitanya Mahāprabhu Himself did.
>
> (Cc. *Mādhya* 11.176)

The preaching orders are perfectly clear, and only a rascal, bogus disciple would desert the active field. Staying alone and avoiding sinful life is certainly not harmful and is superior to material life, but active service is better. Śrīla Prabhupāda once compared the silent meditators to naughty children who at least have been convinced to sit down in one place and stop causing mischief. All materialistic persons are actually causing mischief within God's creation as they passionately go about their sinful, destructive ways. When a parent sees that a child's business is only causing mischief, he may sometimes order the child, "Just sit down in the corner. Don't do anything. Don't move." So the meditator is superior to the mischievous child, but he is not much better than the child who is just sitting silently and doing nothing. But when the child actually improves in consciousness, then he may become active in a productive way for his own welfare and for the benefit of his family. Similarly, the active transcendentalist who acts on behalf of Kṛṣṇa will never commit mischief and is always superior to he who, either out of lack of concern or out of inability, has retired from worldly affairs. If one is entirely incapable of taking part in any preaching activity, then one should certainly save oneself by at least fully engaging in the spiritual principles of chanting and hearing. But it is more pleasing to Kṛṣṇa if one chants and hears and also distributes that chanting by participating in the mission of Kṛṣṇa consciousness.

There is a rare and exalted class of Vaiṣṇavas like Haridāsa Ṭhākura, Raghunātha dāsa Gosvāmī, Jagannātha dāsa Bābājī and Gaurakiśora dāsa Bābāji, who mostly stayed in solitary places and chanted the Hare Kṛṣṇa *mantra*. Their examples of austerity and appreciation for the holy name are so sublime that they are great preachers by example. But they should not be imitated.

There is always scope and strength to be found in the solitary practices of Kṛṣṇa consciousness, such as *japa* and reading. There is also something to be said about occasionally taking time to be alone. Managers who make many decisions involving other people and preachers who mix constantly with the nondevotees should set aside a peaceful time to think of Kṛṣṇa in order to better enact their work on His behalf. But the time of being alone should be balanced or scheduled. Every devotee has his own quota of preaching work, and it should not be avoided.

To me, therefore, the Prahlāda Mahārāja verse is a constant reminder. It is not like a threatening "Big Brother," but it is the Absolute Truth. That truth may sometimes be painful to one who is in a selfish state of consciousness; nevertheless, that truth should be heard and followed. Only then can the masses of conditioned souls get the opportunity to go back to Godhead.

II
Do or Die

dehino 'smin yathā dehe
kaumāraṁ yauvanaṁ jarā
tathā dehāntara-prāptir
dhīras tatra na muhyati

"As the embodied soul continuously passes, in this body, from boyhood to youth to old age, the soul similarly passes into another body at death. A sober person is not bewildered by such a change."

(Bg. 2.13)

"How can you say that!" the young man challenged. "How can you say the self doesn't change? It *does*!" The visitor, a typical Lower East Side American hippie, sat near me on the floor. About thirty other people were also seated facing Prabhupāda, who sat on the raised dais. It was an evening program, and Prabhupāda was taking questions after his lecture on *Bhagavad-gītā*. He had been explaining the meaning of the *dehino 'smin* verse: the body goes through changes from boyhood to youth to old age, but "I," the spirit self, remain the same throughout those changes.

"It's just not true! *I* have changed. I have actually changed, not just my body. Like, before I took LSD, I was a *different* consciousness. No, man, I can't accept that. My identity is changing."

Prabhupāda pointed out that the man had said "my"

identity, implying that he was the same person, but only covered in different ways. In a child's body he had had a child's consciousness. Later he had a young man's consciousness or sometimes an LSD consciousness. But the sense of "I," the awareness of self, remains, whether for the young, old, or deranged.

"No. No way." The rebel stuck to his guns. I could empathize with his point of view; I had also doubted like that. I understood what he meant. But I saw that he did not really understand what Prabhupāda, speaking on behalf of Lord Kṛṣṇa, had meant.

I had come to accept that the self is permanent, and I felt sorry that the visitor could not take it. There was no way he would become Kṛṣṇa conscious unless he accepted the *dehino 'smin* conclusion. In the tension of this challenge to Śrīla Prabhupāda, I felt my own loyalty and conviction aroused. I thought, "This guy is just stuck in his own mental perception of the self," and I knew that there were many others like him. Often guests would hear Prabhupāda's ideas, consider them for a little while, and then reject them. It happened night after night; they would go on living their lives in the temporary, bodily concept, without definite answers.

Later that evening some of us tried talking more with the challenger, but he had other things to do, other places to go. After he had left, a few of the devotees talked about the qualifications for accepting and realizing transcendental knowledge. It is not just a matter of logic or scholarship but requires service to the *guru* and hearing with submission.

It was not unusual for Prabhupāda's dissertations on this verse to provoke discussions. Right from the start it separates the aspiring transcendentalists from the die-hard agnostics. If there is no spirit soul within the body, then everything is only a mass of ignorance, a lump of dead matter created by "chance" in a universal void. We who were following Śrīla Prabhupāda had heard him sufficiently to at least accept the basic presentation of Lord Kṛṣṇa: *ahaṁ brahmāsmi,* "I am not this body." Prabhupāda had stressed it from the very first day. And under his guidance we were at least convinced that it was a worthwhile, serious program to go on reading and hearing and trying to understand the message of *Bhagavad-gītā*.

"How do you accept that there is transmigration of the soul in the next life?" Advaita dāsa asked me. This was no formal inquiry in a lecture hall, but a confidential, personal encounter with an honest brother. We were walking through the streets of the Lower East Side on our way to an afternoon of chanting in Tompkins Square Park. Advaita was a new devotee. He wanted to know why I believed and how he could believe in the soul. I replied in the same, natural way that he had inquired in by giving an example which Śrīla Prabhupāda had given.

"Just like the mother is the one to tell you who your father is. You can't speculate on your own."

He had heard it before, but he knew it was meaningful. "You mean because Swamiji and the *Gītā* are saying it's so?"

"Yes. Otherwise, how can anybody know?"

And that was that. We went to the park and chanted all afternoon.

After Śrīla Prabhupāda left to open the temple in San Francisco, we devotees tried out our new-found, transcendental knowledge by lecturing ourselves. In our lectures, the first words we spoke were usually something involving "You're not this body." And when a few other devotees and I went to Boston, we divided up the morning and evening lectures so that everyone got a chance to repeat the analogies and examples spoken by Lord Kṛṣṇa and Prabhupāda. One devotee even complained, "Always the same lectures, 'You're not this body.' Doesn't anyone know something more?" Actually, most of us did not know much more. Yet even the ABC's of spiritual knowledge were far beyond any knowledge realized by ninety-nine percent of humanity, including all of the prize-winning scholars and religionists. As Śrīla Prabhupāda said, "How simply, how easily explained, but this simple thing they cannot understand."

Kṛṣṇa consciousness is based not on sentiment or speculation but on transcendental knowledge. It is the science of the soul, the science of God. And this verse in the *Bhagavad-gītā* has always represented for me the basic foundation of transcendental knowledge. Transmigration of the soul is not just a nice idea, a wish, or a poetic metaphor. It is a fact. And Śrīla Prabhupāda would often use this verse in that way, as scientific proof. In the analogy used by Lord Kṛṣṇa, the soul remains steady through the changes of body in this lifetime. We should therefore accept the fact that death will be only another change, after which the permanent soul will transmigrate once again.

But different questions or doubts sometimes arise. As the visitor challenged, "My self is not permanent even within this lifetime. *I, myself,* am actually changing from boyhood to youth." And what is the empirical proof that the self does survive the body and take another birth? The Vaiṣṇava *siddhānta* is competent to answer these doubts.

The proof of the soul is not offered empirically, because it lies beyond the ability of the senses or materially speculative mind. The proof descends from a reliable authority:

> As far as the soul's existence is concerned, no one can establish his existence experimentally beyond the proof of *śruti,* or Vedic wisdom. We have to accept this truth, because there is no other source of understanding the existence of the soul, although it is a fact by perception.
>
> (Bg. 2.25, purport)

In the case of the *dehino 'smin* verse, the authority is Śrī Kṛṣṇa, who is accepted in all Vedic literature and by all the bona fide *ācāryas* throughout the ages as the Supreme Personality of Godhead. Because it is spoken by Kṛṣṇa, it is therefore an axiomatic truth. But it is also a fact confirmed by observation, compelling logic, and analogy.

Medical scientists inform us that all of one's body's cells are replaced every seven years. We see that when the lease on one's apartment runs out, one must then take a new place of residence. And when one's clothes become old and worn, one must select new clothing. We see that our bodies do grow from tiny infant bodies to boyhood bodies. And when one is in a body of boyhood, where is the body of his infancy? It is gone; he has changed bodies. Yet his sense of self, of identity, remains. That same self will inevitably change to another body in old age. These are the arguments and examples by which to present the knowledge of the transmigration of the soul. Based on the undeniable fact of the changing body, Lord Kṛṣṇa states that a sober person is not bewildered to know that after death he will continue, and he will take a new body.

How is it that one who was not raised believing in the knowledge of transmigration comes to accept it as axiomatic truth? The enemies of Kṛṣṇa consciousness sometimes call this "brainwashing" or "snapping," indicating that no sane, reasonable process could lead one to such a conversion. More polite and liberal critics of spiritual life say that a devotee's acceptance of Lord Kṛṣṇa's authority is dogmatic or an act of blind faith. The nondevotee's attempt to assess spiritual knowledge is like a person's trying to taste honey by licking the outside of the honey jar. The Kṛṣṇa conscious person, however, asserts that such nonbelievers simply do not know what they are talking about.

I have already given some of the arguments for transmigration, and I have mentioned the basis of accepting transcendental knowledge by hearing from higher authority. Just how a devotee actually becomes transformed in his thinking from "normal," worldly consciousness to Kṛṣṇa consciousness is what I am attempting to explain in these essays. But from the Kṛṣṇa conscious point of view, it is do or die — one accepts this authority and the conclusion of the *dehino 'smin* verse, or his spiritual life dies. Spiritual education may start with intelligent doubt, grow into theoretical acceptance, and finally manifest in firm realization, but if one flatly denies the method of learning from the scriptures, there is no hope.

III
The Constant Companion

hare kṛṣṇa hare kṛṣṇa
kṛṣṇa kṛṣṇa hare hare
hare rāma hare rāma
rāma rāma hare hare

iti ṣoḍaśakaṁ nāmnāṁ
kali-kalmaṣa-nāśanam
nātaḥ parataropāyaḥ
sarva-vedeṣu dṛśyate

"After searching through all the Vedic literature, one cannot find a method of religion more sublime for this age than the chanting of Hare Kṛṣṇa."

(Cc. *Ādi* 3.40)

The first night I saw and heard Śrīla Prabhupāda chanting Hare Kṛṣṇa, I also joined in along with the others in the Lower East Side storefront. I did not know that the *mantra* was a verse from the Upaniṣads. Nor did I know what a *mantra* was, but I thought it a wonderful and exciting meditation.

I had not quite memorized all thirty-two syllables of the chant when I returned home later that evening. But it went on reverberating in my mind as I walked back to my dismal apartment on Suffolk Street: "Hare Kṛṣṇa, Hare Kṛṣṇa, Hare Rāma, Hare Rāma . . ." I had been repainting the walls of my apartment, and when I got home I returned to my painting work. And I also went on singing Hare Kṛṣṇa. After chanting for almost an hour, I sat down to write a letter to a professor friend in Europe. In a light-hearted and carefree way, I explained to him my discovery of the chanting, and I wrote about the Swami and the boys in the storefront. From then on I never missed an evening's chanting meeting at Swamiji's, and I went on chanting to myself wherever I went.

One day I tested myself with a challenge: could I chant for one full hour without stopping? I walked all the way to Fourteenth Street and back, chanting nonstop. Yes, I could chant in a sustained way. I would also chant within my mind while at work in the welfare office.

As time passed and I got to know Śrīla Prabhupāda better, my appreciation of the Hare Kṛṣṇa *mantra* deepened. I found that chanting offered more bliss and satisfaction and shelter than I could even imagine. The *mahā-mantra* had become my constant companion.

The theme of this book is that a devotee lives with the scriptures. Individual verses are like living personalities who guide us as our well-wishing friends. Of all of the millions of Sanskrit verses comprising the Vedic literatures, this verse, the Hare Kṛṣṇa *mantra,* is the dearmost companion of all. In this sense the Hare Kṛṣṇa verse, or the Hare Kṛṣṇa *mantra,* is unique. Even though we study many verses and purports and memorize a number of them, the Hare Kṛṣṇa *mantra* is the supreme well-wisher, and He is every devotee's special protector. Even if one knew no other verses but simply chanted this verse constantly, he could attain pure Kṛṣṇa consciousness.

This verse is for all seasons and for all moods. When we are afraid, we chant Hare Kṛṣṇa; when we confront a problem, this verse comes to our mind and lips; when we are happy or tired, when we distribute a book or answer the telephone, we pray with this verse. When we get an opportunity to speak to a large audience, such as on radio or television, we never forget to say Hare Kṛṣṇa at least once. And when we meet our friends in devotional service, we recite this verse as a greeting.

None of the sastric *ślokas* are ordinary letter combinations; they are all nondifferent from Kṛṣṇa. This is particularly emphasized, however, in reference to the Hare Kṛṣṇa *mantra:* Hare Kṛṣṇa, Hare Kṛṣṇa, Kṛṣṇa Kṛṣṇa, Hare Hare/ Hare Rāma, Hare Rāma, Rāma Rāma, Hare Hare. Lord Kṛṣṇa Himself is with us on our tongue when we chant His holy name. And for us, the words *japa* and *kīrtana* refer exclusively to different methods of reciting and meditating upon this verse. In *japa,* we engage our tongue and ear by reciting the *mahā-mantra* continuously, and we turn inward to meditate on the holy name of Kṛṣṇa. *Japa* beads are not for counting repetitions of any other verse. *Kīrtana* means *kṛṣṇa-kīrtana,* the chanting of the holy names, the Hare Kṛṣṇa *mantra.* During *kīrtanas* within the temple we dance and play instruments in a transcendental festival, and we experience congregational unity within the holy name. We are a family whose essence is service to the holy name. In public *kīrtana,* we share *hari-nāma* and distribute it to the reluctant nondevotees. In such sometimes wild and uncontrollable situations we simultaneously distribute Hare Kṛṣṇa while ourselves taking shelter in the Lord's internal energy through His sound vibration.

Just as all sastric verses must be given and explained in *paramparā,* so the Hare Kṛṣṇa *mantra* comes to us from Śrīla Prabhupāda. Otherwise, it would have remained an obscure verse within the *Upaniṣads,* one of many *bhajanas* or *mantras* within the grab-bag of the so-called "swamis" and hodgepodge "bhaktas" of India. But Śrīla Prabhupāda has delivered to us the holy name with the *paramparā* conclusions of Lord Caitanya. In effect, Śrīla Prabhupāda has said,

"Please chant Hare Kṛṣṇa, and make this chanting your constant companion. Then even at the time of death you will have nothing to fear." On his order we therefore practice and try to realize that this verse is Kṛṣṇa Himself, our dearmost friend.

In one sense, there is no translation of the Hare Kṛṣṇa *mantra*, since it is made up of proper nouns. The *mantra* is the constant calling on the names of God: Hare, Kṛṣṇa, and Rāma; the call does not need to be translated. When the child cries "Mother! Mother!" one may analyze the meaning if one wishes, but the simple meaning is nondifferent from the cry itself. And yet, the spiritual masters have translated the verse to mean, "O Supreme Lord, O energy of the Lord! Please engage me in Your service!" The chanting of Hare Kṛṣṇa is not an attempt to relate to the Lord by the mechanical repetition of His name. Rather, we are petitioning Him to please keep us at His lotus feet and to please allow us the privilege of engaging as the menial servant of His servant. The special benediction of this absolute prayer is that its recitation is itself the topmost form of service to Lord Kṛṣṇa in this age. By His causeless mercy, Lord Kṛṣṇa has consented to be everyone's most intimate companion in the form of the most beloved of all verses, Hare Kṛṣṇa, Hare Kṛṣṇa, Kṛṣṇa Kṛṣṇa, Hare Hare/ Hare Rāma, Hare Rāma, Rāma Rāma, Hare Hare.

Since my initial good fortune in receiving the holy name from Śrīla Prabhupāda, I have gone on to chant a regulated but often uninspired routine of sixteen rounds daily. I have described my attempt to battle against offensive chanting in *Japa Reform Notebook*. Unfortunately, I continue to move along in some of the same old ruts of inattention and many-branched distraction while chanting the holy name. Of course, we say, "It is a gradual process." There is always great hope that when I go to chant again I will improve. But *japa* reform is a constant, continual struggle, and victory against the demons of offensive chanting is not so easily won.

With time, as we prepare ourselves for the oncoming, most dangerous moment of death, we better understand that the holy name is our ultimate shelter. If indeed it will take us more than one lifetime to attain pure chanting, then our prayer is to somehow be born where we may take up the *māhā-mantra* once again, whether in heaven or hell. This much we have already learned: the chanting is our constant companion, our life and soul, our matchless gift from Śrīla Prabhupāda.

IV
Remembering Kṛṣṇa When in Trouble

tat te 'nukampāṁ susamīkṣamāṇo
bhuñjāna evātma-kṛtam vipākam
hṛd-vāg-vapurbhir vidadhan namas te
jīveta yo mukti-pade sa dāya-bhāk

"My dear Lord, one who constantly waits for Your causeless mercy to be bestowed upon him and who goes on suffering the reactions of his past misdeeds, offering You respectful obeisances from the core of his heart, is surely eligible for liberation, for it has become his rightful claim."

(*Bhāg.* 10.14.8)

"This statement," Śrīla Prabhupāda writes in *The Nectar of Devotion*, ". . . should be the guide for all devotees." (NOD, p.91) This is a case where Śrīla Prabhupāda has pointed to a specific verse and told us to live with it and to let it be our constant guide. "When impediments arise," he writes, "we should simply think of Kṛṣṇa and expect His mercy. That is the only solace."

Śrīla Prabhupāda also personally recommended this verse to me in a letter of August 1971. The letter arose out of a discussion among the devotees in the Boston temple. We were puzzled as to why devotees suffer. If the devotees are free from *karma*, what then is the cause of the sufferings and reverses which sometimes afflict the devotee community? And if this suffering is not *karma*, then is it the direct action of the Supreme? I wrote to Śrīla Prabhupāda on behalf of the devotees in the Boston temple, and I received his reply shortly thereafter:

> Once surrendered to Krsna, karmic reaction is immediately gone. But if he again acts independently, then he is again in the clutches of maya. That marginal state is always there. But for the pure devotee who is actually surrendered to Krsna, he has no karmic reaction. The example is given of the fan switched off. It is still running some rounds, but that will be stopped very soon. That is his position. Therefore a pure devotee who is having some adverse reaction, he doesn't take ill of it. He knows that the karmic reaction is already stopped but what is happening is the residual turning of the fan, even after the switch is off. A pure devotee therefore takes it as the mercy of the Lord because the Lord is finishing his karmic reaction by summary punishment.
>
> Tat te 'nukampam susamiksamano. To the devotee such adverse condition is seen as the mercy of the Lord and more enthusiastically he engages himself in the Lord's transcendental service. He is never hampered by such reactions. Neither his Krsna consciousness is not hampered by the least degree. In the presence of such adverse conditions of karmic reaction the Lord advises to tolerate.
>
> Tams titiksasva bharata: "My dear Arjuna, please tolerate these things without being perplexed. They come and go like seasonal changes of summer and winter. They have nothing to do with the pure soul engaged in devotional service." So the reaction is stopped but the momentum is still there. Simply one has to tolerate.

We regarded this letter as an amazing and rare piece of evidence, as if its points were not stated elsewhere in the scriptures. Prabhupāda had completely cleared up the philosophical question once and for all: a devotee does not suffer *karma* but only a residual or leftover reaction from his past. It is not a fresh reaction, because he has no new sins and because the toll of his past sins has been removed by his initiation into spiritual life by a bona fide spiritual master. The suffering is a spinning of the fan with the plug pulled out. It is a summary or token punishment and should not affect the devotee's determination to serve. Yet for some of the Boston devotees another question remained: "Prabhupāda says that this instruction is for a pure devotee, so we still do not know if it applies to us. I know that *I* am not a pure devotee!" But this question seems to be answered also. The words "once surrendered" mean the stage when we accept the spiritual master and when we vow to abide by the rules of Kṛṣṇa consciousness—avoiding the four kinds of sinful activities, chanting sixteen rounds of the Hare Kṛṣṇa *mantra* daily, and engaging in full devotional service. If, due to our marginal nature, *we again sin,* then we again place the plug back into the powerhouse of *māyā* and accrue karmic reaction. But as long as we actually follow, then we qualify for being "pure devotees," at least in the preliminary sense. Such a devotee tolerates reverses, goes on with his service to Kṛṣṇa, and is free of karmic reaction. So the philosophy is clear, but we have to live it.

This is a major verse to reflect on when we are in physical or mental pain, when we become lost or lose a lot of money, or when we are threatened by a great calamity or other awkward, human embarrassments. I cannot exactly remember whether in times of distress I have actually thought of this Sanskrit verse and its English translation. I do know that I usually think of the words "Hare Kṛṣṇa!" and I think, "All right, this is it—trouble. Now think of Kṛṣṇa." Sometimes I tell myself, "This bad turn is really good, because it will make me detached." And I know that some devotees at such times think of the brave words of Queen Kunti, who said, "I wish that all those calamities would happen again and again so that we could see You again and again, for seeing You means that we will no longer see repeated births and deaths." (*Bhāg.* 1.8.25) Other devotional thoughts that may come in times of distress include: "If this is what Kṛṣṇa wants, then let it happen," and "We are not these bodies. Only by illusion do we think we are in danger." These and similar thoughts may be seen as corollaries to this great verse of the *Śrīmad-Bhāgavatam,* which begins *tat te 'nukampām,* and which teaches us much about life and about our relationship with God.

There *is* God, Kṛṣṇa, and yet there *is* suffering. Our suffering is due to our breaking the laws of nature. When we eat too much we get sick, and when we touch fire we get burned. These are the laws of nature. Everyone who is born into this world has foolishly desired to leave Kṛṣṇa and come here, where there are such hard and fast laws at every turn. We come and stay here and inevitably break these laws, causing suffering to others and to ourselves. That is our foolish wish. Kṛṣṇa, however, wants us to revive our memory of Him and return to Him and the spiritual world. He wants us to end the illusion by which we think we can be happy in material life.

In this verse, Lord Kṛṣṇa describes the enlightened response to suffering: he who never blames God, who is not bewildered when facing a reverse in life, who knows that things are happening according to the workings of one's own *karma* and yet thinks of Kṛṣṇa favorably, he gains the greatest freedom, even in suffering. As Prabhupāda writes in *The Nectar of Devotion,* "If a devotee passes his days in that spirit, it is certain that he is going to be promoted to the abode of the Lord. By such activities he earns his claim to enter into the kingdom of God." (NOD, p.91)

There is a sweet relationship described here. The devotee has not always been a devotee; he has been a rascal and has committed many impious acts. But by the grace of the Lord and by the grace of the Lord's pure devotee, the sinner has now become a devotee, although he feels himself unfit.

By his humble patience in the face of adversity, a devotee wins the favor of the Lord, who is arranging to take him back to Godhead.

The material world is a place of sadness because it is full of suffering. But in this *tat te 'nukampām* verse the Lord is inspiring His devotee. And there are many such devotees, both in the past and in the present, who have adopted this inspired attitude toward their sufferings. The relationship described in this verse is made up of the devotee's patience and the forgiveness of Kṛṣṇa, who is taking His devotee back to the spiritual world. This relationship can only be understood by the pure devotee. Impious persons become atheists when in distressful conditions. As Śrīla Prabhupāda writes in *The Nectar of Devotion,* "Because he doesn't firmly believe in God, he thinks he can adjust his distressed condition by totally disbelieving Him." But the faithfulness of the devotee, especially while enduring difficult times, earns him the right to return to the spiritual world.

V
A Song About Kṛṣṇaloka

cintāmaṇi-prakara-sadmasu kalpa-vṛkṣa-
lakṣāvṛteṣu surabhīr abhipālayantam
lakṣmī-sahasra-śata-sambrama-sevyamānaṁ
govindam ādi-puruṣaṁ tam ahaṁ bhajāmi

"I worship Govinda, the primal Lord, the first progenitor, who is tending the cows, fulfilling all desires, in abodes built with spiritual gems, surrounded by millions of purpose trees, always served with great reverence and affection by hundreds of thousands of *lakṣmīs* or *gopīs*."

(*Brahma-saṁhitā* 5.29)

I was sitting with Śrīla Prabhupāda in his room at 26 Second Avenue one evening when he suddenly gave me this verse. Because I could not understand the Sanskrit, he had to pronounce and spell each word, which I would write down. When I finished writing the verse and its English translation, I asked Śrīla Prabhupāda what it was. He said, "It is a song about Kṛṣṇaloka." I typed the verse and we then included it in a collection of prayers which Prabhupāda had given us. For years, the verse was known simply as "A Song About Kṛṣṇaloka." It stood as a small, complete poem. We did not know it was one of over sixty verses from the *Brahma-saṁhitā*.

In 1969, Prabhupāda made a long-playing record which featured Prabhupāda singing this and other verses from the

Brahma-saṁhitā. Also included on the album was a spoken explanation of the *cintāmaṇi* verse. Much of this talk was taken directly from the texts and purports of the *Brahma-saṁhitā* as published by Bhaktisiddhānta Sarasvatī Ṭhākura following the commentaries of Jīva Gosvāmī. Prabhupāda's first words after singing are as follows:

> The materialistic demeanor cannot possibly stretch to the Transcendental Autocrat who is ever inviting the fallen conditioned souls to associate with Him through devotion or eternal serving mood.

Prabhupāda was later to say that ninety-five percent of the philosophy of Kṛṣṇa consciousness is included in that recorded speech.

In his purport to this *cintāmaṇi* verse, Śrīla Bhaktisiddhānta Sarasvatī describes the thinking of the materialistic mental speculator as well as the special qualification of one who would truly benefit from hearing the verses of the *Brahma-saṁhitā:*

> For want of a taste of things spiritual, a grave doubt arises in the minds of those who are enchained by worldly knowledge. On hearing a narration of the pastimes of Kṛṣṇa, they think that the truth [*tattva*] regarding Kṛṣṇa is a mental concoction of certain learned scholars created by their imaginative brains out of material drawn from the mundane principles. With the object of removing this harmful doubt, Brahmā in this and the following *ślokas*, after distinguishing between the two things, viz. spirit and matter, in a rational manner has tried to make one understand the pure *līlā* of Kṛṣṇa, obtained by his unmixed, ecstatic trance.
>
> (*Brahma-saṁhitā*, 5.32, purport)

Although rational, Lord Brahmā's descriptions reveal a realm which is inconceivable by ordinary methods of perception. These descriptions of Kṛṣṇaloka meet the standard of *śāstra* because they are directly revealed to Brahmā by

Lord Kṛṣṇa. They comprise perfect knowledge revealed by the all-perfect Supreme Lord. I have personally regarded the *cintāmaṇi* verse in this way ever since receiving it from Śrīla Prabhupāda. I did not question the sastric origins of this verse or feel the need to consult other sources to verify its authenticity. Because it was presented to me by my spiritual master, I accepted it as a true picture, "a song about Kṛṣṇaloka." Since receiving this verse from Śrīla Prabhupāda, it has to me remained a direct manifestation of Lord Kṛṣṇa in His eternal abode. This description of Kṛṣṇaloka is the realized expression (*vijñāna*) of Lord Brahmā, and to the degree that we receive this verse with submissive devotion, we can also directly perceive the Supreme Lord's place, person, associates, and paraphernalia in the eternal world. This need for a devotional attitude in attaining knowledge of Kṛṣṇa is expressed in another verse from the *Brahma-saṁhitā:*

> I worship Govinda, the primal Lord, who is Śyāmasundara, Kṛṣṇa Himself, with inconceivable, innumerable attributes, whom the pure devotees see in their heart of hearts with the eye of devotion tinged with the salve of love.
>
> (*Brahma-saṁhitā* 5.38)

By serving Śrīla Prabhupāda and by hearing from him with full faith, we can progressively gain appreciation and conviction about the transcendental nature of Kṛṣṇa in His *cintāmaṇi-dhāma.*

If someone challenges, "How do you know?" and for reply a devotee says, "I heard it from the authoritative source," then the challenge is rightly answered. As I once replied to my Godbrother Advaita dāsa when he asked me a similar question, we learn the truth by hearing, as the son learns of the identity of his father by hearing from his mother. If sometimes I feel very removed from Kṛṣṇa conscious realization, or if I become forgetful of the real goal of all activities, I remember this verse and the principle of realization by hearing. Although I am certainly poor-hearted, I *do* know Kṛṣṇaloka, I *do* know the abode of the Supreme Lord, because I have heard a detailed description of it in the song of Kṛṣṇaloka.

A skeptic may refuse my realization, but he cannot deny me entrance into the transcendental abode of Kṛṣṇa. By the grace of my spiritual master, I have not rejected Kṛṣṇa's offer of spiritual knowledge, and so I do not remain in ignorance of the Absolute Truth. I may be questioned, "But do you really know the *cintāmaṇi-dhāma,* or are you just saying you accept the scripture's description of it?" My reply is that regardless of the degree or amount I may realize, nevertheless I know it. How much I may appreciate or know is my own situation. But the abode is a fact. The place, *Vṛndāvana-dhāma,* is there. Kṛṣṇa is there, and the *surabhi* are there. The narration is factual.

Kṛṣṇa conscious artists, guided by *guru, śāstra,* and *sādhu,* have painted many scenes of Lord Kṛṣṇa and His associates in Kṛṣṇaloka. Their paintings are like open windows to the spiritual sky, and they further help us to see Kṛṣṇa even with our present eyes. One picture shows Kṛṣṇa returning from the pasturing grounds with innumerable attractive *surabhi* cows, while the affectionate cowherd boys surround Him, and the yearning *gopīs,* who have been waiting all day to see Kṛṣṇa return, gather on the roofs and at the doorways of their homes to greet their returning hero. I once described this picture in a poem:

Govinda is coming home,
Balarāma too,
with flute and plow.
They walk the blessed earth
surrounded by cows.
Green-brown Vṛndāvana
trees enrich the air,
birds singing,

frolicking beauty;
but only confidential servants
live there.

The worship of the Rādhā-Kṛṣṇa Deities also affords us a direct view of the highest worshipful *rasa* of Kṛṣṇa and His dearmost devotee. Kṛṣṇa is very merciful to come and reveal His pastimes, but it is up to the individual devotee, guided by his *guru,* to approach Him in a serving mood. When Kṛṣṇa manifested Himself in Vṛndāvana five thousand years ago, both the devotees and the nondevotees could see Him, but only the devotees cherished Him. Even today Kṛṣṇa is fully presenting Himself through His teachings and pastimes, but it is only by virtue of a pure heart that the devotee can perceive and appreciate Kṛṣṇa and His *dhāma.* But it is also true that Lord Kṛṣṇa helps us to approach Him:

> To those who are constantly devoted to serving Me with love, I give the understanding by which they can come to Me. To show them special mercy, I, dwelling in their hearts, destroy with the shining lamp of knowledge the darkness born of ignorance.
>
> (Bg. 10.10–11)

Aside from the material vision which prevents us from seeing and appreciating Kṛṣṇa, practicing devotees sometimes feel that the pressure of their duties to the spiritual master makes it difficult for them to concentrate on Kṛṣṇaloka. This "problem" is addressed by the first essay in this book, "The Devotee Is a Preacher." We will never be able to concentrate on Kṛṣṇaloka if we stop performing the duties given to us by the spiritual master or if we attempt to sit down in a secluded place to chant and to think exclusively about Kṛṣṇa. But by taking up the spirit of serving the *guru's* order and fighting against the propaganda of the atheists, we please Kṛṣṇa. And only by pleasing Him through sincere acts of devotional service can we understand Kṛṣṇa in Vṛndāvana. As Śrīla Prabhupāda used to say,

"Don't try to see Kṛṣṇa, but act in such a way that Kṛṣṇa can see you." As intensely preoccupying as they may be, our spiritual duties for spreading Kṛṣṇa consciousness within this world do not prevent or distract us from concentrating on the descriptions of Kṛṣṇaloka. Rather, they qualify us to one day realize Vṛndāvana.

"Deserve, then desire," Śrīla Prabhupāda said. A selfish desire to enjoy the fruits of the spiritual world will not qualify us for returning to *cintāmaṇi-dhāma*. We have to deserve. One goes to Kṛṣṇaloka to be a cowherd friend of Kṛṣṇa only after performing heaps and volumes of pious devotional activities. In time, as we become qualified, the *dhāma* will be revealed to us. And even now, at every step in our devotional service, we are never without Kṛṣṇa provided we desire to please Him. His holy name is ever-ready to accept our service in chanting. His Deity form stands on the altar in the temple, agreeable and compliant to our service of dressing Him, cooking for Him, and bowing down at His lotus feet. And prayers like the *cintāmaṇi* song are ours to sing.

We are advised while in this world to develop the mentality of a wife who has a paramour. Such a wife performs her household duties faithfully, so as not to arouse suspicion, yet she always thinks of the time when she can be free to go to her lover. Our worldly duties should be kept to a minimum, and we should appreciate that all of our spiritual duties are freeing us of material desires and qualifying us to attain that pure state in which Kṛṣṇa reveals Himself through His devotee.

But why should we ever be without thought of Kṛṣṇa in Kṛṣṇaloka? In concluding his recorded *cintāmaṇi* talk, Śrīla Prabhupāda requests his hearers "to study and try to enter into the spirit of this hymn with great care and attention as a regular daily function."

VI
Removing the Material Veil

anāsaktasya viṣayān
yathārham upayuñjataḥ
nirbandhaḥ kṛṣṇa-sambandhe
yuktaṁ vairāgyam ucyate

prāpañcikatayā buddhyā
hari-sambandhi-vastunaḥ
mumukṣubhiḥ parityāgo
vairāgyaṁ phalgu kathyate

"When one is not attached to anything, but at the same time accepts everything in relation to Kṛṣṇa, one is rightly situated above possessiveness. On the other hand, one who rejects everything without knowledge of its relationship to Kṛṣṇa is not complete in his renunciation.

(*Bhakti-rasāmṛta-sindhu* 2.225–56)

It was a summer afternoon in 1966. Śrīla Prabhupāda sat behind his little trunk which doubled as his desk in his apartment at 26 Second Avenue. "Actually," Śrīla Prabhupāda was saying, "everything is spiritual if it is used in Kṛṣṇa's service." With his hand he indicated the nearby black telephone as an object of potential spirituality. This amazed me at once. Śrīla Prabhupāda's words changed everything. I had thought of the "spiritual" as an inconceivable, imperceptible realm, but Śrīla Prabhupāda showed me that in the dynamism of Kṛṣṇa consciousness, the pure devotee sees the whole world in relation to Kṛṣṇa, as His energy. And he uses everything in His service. Although I could not falsely adopt Śrīla Prabhupāda's pure, expansive consciousness, on first hearing his explanation I could nevertheless foresee an exciting future, and I could appreciate with a fresh wonder that Śrīla Prabhupāda did not see the same old, tired world of matter that everyone else saw.

Once, on a New York television show, a panel member asked Śrīla Prabhupāda, "If you have renounced material things, why do you mark your forehead with clay and play brass cymbals while you sing?" Prabhupāda replied that clay used for Vaiṣṇava markings and musical instruments used to chant the Hare Kṛṣṇa *mantra* were not material things, but spiritual. He said it is a question of one's consciousness and that, factually speaking, everything comes from Kṛṣṇa, who is all-spiritual. Śrīla Prabhupāda's answer met with a stunned, appreciative response. It defeated the idea that the spiritual world is made up only of air or noncorporeal light. The transformation of the whole material world into spirit suddenly loomed as practical reality when revealed by the words of Kṛṣṇa's pure devotee.

As Śrīla Prabhupāda explains in a *Bhagavad-gītā* purport, "The material veil can be removed at once by Kṛṣṇa consciousness. . . . The Absolute Truth covered by *māyā* is called matter. Matter dovetailed for the cause of the Absolute Truth regains its spiritual quality." (Bg. 4.24, purport)

The die-hard materialist rejects this transformation process by challenging that the devotee is simply exploiting matter for his own enjoyment like everyone else. Śrīla Prabhupāda refutes the materialist's point in *The Nectar of Devotion*, where he explains "a secret of devotional service":

> Sometimes people ask us, "Why are you utilizing material products if you condemn the advancement of material civilization?" But actually we do not condemn. We simply

> ask people to do whatever they are doing in Kṛṣṇa consciousness. This is the same principle on which, in *Bhagavad-gītā,* Kṛṣṇa advised Arjuna to utilize his fighting abilities in devotional service. Similarly, we are utilizing these machines for Kṛṣṇa's service. With such sentiment for Kṛṣṇa, or Kṛṣṇa consciousness, we can accept everything. If the typewriter can be utilized for advancing our Kṛṣṇa consciousness movement, we must accept it. Similarly the dictating machine or any other machine must be used. Our vision is that Kṛṣṇa is everything. Kṛṣṇa is the cause and effect, and nothing belongs to us. Kṛṣṇa's things must be used in the service of Kṛṣṇa. That is our vision.
>
> (*The Nectar of Devotion,* p.115

Once the devotees took Śrīla Prabhupāda on a tour of the factory which produced incense for ISKCON's newly prospering Spiritual Sky incense business. While looking through an office window down into a spacious warehouse, Śrīla Prabhupāda quoted this *anāsaktasya viṣayān* verse of Rūpa Gosvāmī. At that time none of the devotees knew the meaning of the Sanskrit, but they wrote it down as he spoke it and followed his advice to frame the verse and hang it on the office wall. Later, when Spiritual Sky produced a colorful advertising brochure, a skeptical disciple wrote to Śrīla Prabhupāda, asking, "Isn't this *māyā*?" Prabhupāda replied that anything which makes a million dollars for Kṛṣṇa is not *māyā*. Śrīla Prabhupāda challenged the skeptic, saying, "When will you learn this important point? *Your* idea is *māyā,* because you do not understand that everything may be used—including business and money—in the service of Kṛṣṇa."

Although the first dawning of this realization inspired me, I sometimes failed to appreciate how auspicious it actually is to use everything in Kṛṣṇa's service. In 1971, while attempting to purchase a large building complex in Dallas, Texas, for use as ISKCON's *gurukula,* I faltered and thought I was becoming materially motivated. For half a year the purchase negotiations dragged on, during which time I became more and more involved in arranging for a down payment, studying the mortgage and interest rates, obtaining property assessments, title clearances, and so on. "Is this really spiritual life?" I asked myself. Maybe I was trying so hard to succeed just so I could become famous for purchasing the biggest building in our movement. Maybe it was not good for my spiritual life to be involved in the real estate game. I conveyed some of this doubt and anxiety in a letter to Śrīla Prabhupāda. His reply set me back on the right course:

> There is no question of personal desires. You are a sincere boy and I give you all my blessings to go ahead with this project. Caitanya Mahāprabhu has said that "externally we may behave like ordinary men, but internally we remain fixed in the service of Radha-Krsna." The Mayavadi cannot accept this fact and they take devotional service to be maya; therefore we call them Mayavadis. You should never, however, accept the Mayavadi philosophy, at any time.

This letter made me happy, but it startled me, too. Prabhupāda said I was becoming a Māyāvādī! With renewed zeal, I plunged back into the complex financial and legal exchange with the lawyers and real estate agents, and by Kṛṣṇa's and Prabhupāda's grace, we eventually secured the purchase.

Are there any rules or boundaries governing the transformation of matter into spirit? Can anyone do this and claim that he is spiritual and therefore perfect and beyond criticism? Can we do whatever we like just by saying, "It's for Kṛṣṇa"? Śrīla Prabhupāda clearly answers these questions in a *Bhagavad-gītā* purport:

> One should, however, note that after doing something whimsically he should not offer the result to the Supreme Lord. That sort of duty is not in the devotional service of Krsna consciousness. One should act according to the order

> of Krsna. This is a very important point. That order of Krsna comes through disciplic succession from the bona fide spiritual master. Therefore the spiritual master's order should be taken as the prime duty of life.
>
> (Bg. 18.57, purport)

Under the authorized guidance of *guru* and Kṛṣṇa, a devotee should be enthusiastic to engage all persons and all things in the service of the Lord. The more the activities of the material world are performed in Kṛṣṇa consciousness, the more the world's atmosphere becomes spiritualized. Lord Kṛṣṇa declares, "By Me in My unmanifested form, this entire universe is pervaded." (Bg. 9.4) Therefore, a devotee is not concocting out of his own sentiment when he attempts to make everything favorable for Kṛṣṇa's service. Factually, it is all Kṛṣṇa's energy, and all beings are His parts and parcels; but illusion covers everything in the material world. When Kṛṣṇa's energy is again engaged in His service, then everyone can become peaceful and satisfied in the normal constitutional position as eternal servant of Kṛṣṇa.

The quality of *utsāha,* or enthusiasm in devotional service, is one of the prime factors for advancement in spiritual life. In explaining this quality, Śrīla Prabhupāda cites Rūpa Gosvāmī's verse regarding the devotee who is working to dovetail matter into spirit:

> Endeavor executed with intelligence is called *utsāha,* or enthusiasm. The devotees find the correct means by which everything can be utilized in the service of the Lord (*nirbandhaḥ kṛṣṇa-sambandhe yuktaṁ vairāgyam ucyate.*) The execution of devotional sevice is not a matter of idle meditation but practical action in the foreground of spiritual life.
>
> (*The Nectar of Instruction,* Text 3, purport)

Thus the devotee works intelligently in the practical field to engage everything in Kṛṣṇa's service. How such an attempt to in every way serve Kṛṣṇa leads a devotee into unusual adventures beyond the stereotypes of spiritual life, and how these devotional acts lead him to liberation, are explained in the next essay.

VII
Liberation Despite all Conditions

īhā yasya harer dāsye
karmaṇā manasā girā
nikhilāsv apy avasthāsu
jīvan-muktaḥ sa ucyate

"One who is engaged fully with his body, mind, and speech in the service of the Lord is liberated even within this body, despite his condition."

(*Bhakti-rasāmṛta-sindhu* 1.2.187)

My Godbrother Ghanaśyāma dāsa brahmacārī and I were members of a traveling team distributing Śrīla Prabhupāda's books at the universities. So as not to alarm professors and librarians—who have their own stereotyped idea of how book salesmen should appear—we wore business suits and grew long hair or wore wigs. One freezing winter day, Ghanaśyāma and I found ourselves walking across the campus of the University of Wisconsin in Milwaukee, wearing overcoats we had purchased for two dollars each at a charity store and carrying our heavy book valises. Just as we were about to part company and go knocking on professors' doors, Ghanaśyāma turned to me and said, "Wow! Who would have imagined that spiritual life would be like this?" My Godbrother and I laughed together to find ourselves serving our spiritual master in a way we had never before dreamed of. The contrast between our salesperson's appearance and our actual lives as *brahmacārīs,* as well as the contrast between what we had previously conceived of as spiritual activity and our present, unusual roles, made us both laugh. And the humor was pleasantly sustained by our strong convictions that selling books in Śrīla Prabhupāda's service was genuine spiritual life and that acting in this way liberated us from material desires.

In a similar way, many of Śrīla Prabhupāda's followers find themselves in situations which smash their previously held stereotyped ideas of religious life. Just to be a servant is something most of us never thought of as either spiritual or desirable. A servant, we thought, was a black slave in the pre–Civil War days of America or a hired valet or a traditionally dressed butler as might appear in the Hollywood movies. Who could imagine that being a servant of God—and not even a direct servant but a servant of the servant of the servant of God, one hundred times removed—is actually the highest spiritual position?

Before meeting with Kṛṣṇa consciousness, some of us may have thought that spiritual life must be dry or even boring, and meant fasting or observing vows of silence. If so, we were pleasantly surprised to find that it is filled with festivals and chanting Hare Kṛṣṇa in ecstatic, dancing congregations, and feasting on sumptuously cooked *prasādam.* And upon reading Śrīla Prabhupāda's books, we may have been surprised to find not dry, intellectual wrangling but the delightful pastimes of the Supreme Lord and His associates. The childhood pastimes of Kṛṣṇa in Vṛndāvana are very playful and charming, and Lord Caitanya's pastimes are sometimes humorous, as when His devotees engage in joking or when they play at water sports. And Lord Caitanya's dealings with His devotees are always loving. Śrīla Rūpa Gosvāmī encourages the devotees to engage in exchanges of love with each other by sharing and accepting gifts, by giving and accepting *prasādam,* by revealing their minds intimately, and by hearing the personal revelations of others. Spiritual theater, art, and music, as well as opportunities for wide travel, make for a busy, active life.

The real conclusion of this phenomenon—and it is a triumphant one experienced by every devotee—is that despite the seemingly unusual activities which the Kṛṣṇa conscious devotee may occasionally take on in this world, Kṛṣṇa consciousness is actually liberation from all material affairs. But even if we grant that the Kṛṣṇa conscious devotee is acting on the liberated platform, a big question remains: What do we mean by liberation?

According to Vedic knowledge, liberation (*mukti*) means to become free from the cycle of repeated birth and death. The impersonalist philosophers think that this can be attained through meditation, by which one reaches a stage where one's identity merges into the supreme whole. The *Śrīmad-Bhāgavatam* declares, however, that even if the meditator can merge with the impersonal *brahmajyoti,* he will eventually have to again take birth in a material form due to his lack of a devotional relationship with Kṛṣṇa. As Lord Kṛṣṇa states to Arjuna in the *Bhagavad-gītā,* we are all eternal persons. There was never a time in the past when we did not exist, and as we are existing as persons in the present, so too will we exist as persons in the future. Liberation, therefore, cannot be attained through the attempt to annihilate the self by entering a void or merging with the One. Real liberation occurs when we free ourselves of all material contamination and in the pure devotional state enter into the eternal association of Lord Kṛṣṇa in the spiritual world. And that state of freedom from all material anxiety can be attained even while we are living within this world, as described in the verse under study: "One who is engaged fully with his body, mind and speech in the service of the Lord is liberated even within this body, despite his condition."

Ultimately, liberation is not the goal of spiritual life, but it is an automatic by-product of devotional service. As stated by the Vaiṣṇava saint Śrīla Bilvamaṅgala, "If I have unflinching devotion unto the lotus feet of the Supreme Lord, then *mukti*, or liberation, serves me as my maid-servant." A pure devotee serves the Supreme without any motive; he does not serve the Lord with the motive of some material return or even with the hope that by serving he will become liberated. As Lord Caitanya writes in His *Śikṣāṣṭaka* prayers,

> O almighty Lord, I have no desire for accumulating wealth, nor have I any desire to enjoy beautiful women; neither do I want numbers of followers. What I only want is that I may have Your causeless devotional service in my life, birth after birth.
>
> (*Śikṣāṣṭaka* 4)

Out of humility, the pure devotee does not think himself fit for liberation. He is willing to be born again in the material world, and his only request is that he be allowed to associate with pure devotees and not forget his beloved, the Supreme Personality of Godhead. Although he does not serve for the purpose of going back to Godhead, the pure devotee's mind and activities are so pleasing to Kṛṣṇa that He brings His pure servant to Him for eternal association in the spiritual world.

Although the devotee's services to the spiritual master are multifarious and easily award one liberation, they sometimes bring the devotee into direct conflict with the material world. These occasions provide tests of one's sincerity and trust in Kṛṣṇa consciousness. It is one thing to enjoy the liberated status of devotional service when one's activities provide humorous contrasts to stereotyped ways of life. But when the execution of one's spiritual duties seems to bring one only trouble, the tendency is to have second thoughts and in a different mood ask oneself, "Is this what I came to spiritual life for?"

Once while I was distributing books on a street in Tucson, Arizona, a storeowner assaulted me and broke my *sannyāsa* rod over my head and shoulders. And once while singing in a *kīrtana* at the Boston Commons a thrown bottle hit me in the head. Many devotees have gone to jail for the offense of chanting Hare Kṛṣṇa in public places. While living peacefully in their temples and *āśramas,* devotees have been shot at and bombed. The news media regularly blasphemes and abuses the Kṛṣṇa consciousness movement, and if a devotee decides to dedicate his or her life to Kṛṣṇa consciousness, there is a good chance that he or she will be rejected by family, friends, and society.

Aside from tolerating the negative attitudes, a devotee must be responsible to push on the mission of Kṛṣṇa consciousness in a revolutionary spirit. The Kṛṣṇa consciousness movement is not quietism or mere armchair speculation. It is war against *māyā.* Thus we can understand that liberation does not mean that one simply meditates "I am eternal" and does nothing. When Sanātana Gosvāmī, a learned disciple of Lord Caitanya, approached his master, he inquired, "You have said that I am already liberated; now what are my duties in the liberated state?"

Liberated duties may include arranging for marriage of disciples, providing for the raising and education of children, and struggling to raise funds for conducting and expanding a spiritual movement. One may ask, "Well, how does that differ from material life?"

The answer is that in Kṛṣṇa consciousness, these seemingly material duties are undertaken not for anyone's personal gratification but for the purpose of pleasing Kṛṣṇa. One who willingly undertakes these services and who does not resent the headaches and entanglements which may result from practical devotional service in this world becomes very dear to Kṛṣṇa and enters into an intimate relationship with Kṛṣṇa in the spiritual world.

In an earlier essay, we quoted Prabhupāda's aphorism "Deserve and then desire." One cannot enter into his relationship with Kṛṣṇa and the *gopīs* simply by desiring, but one has to deserve this by the good credits of service unto the spiritual master. Therefore a devotee should never feel sorry if his devotional service leads him into many difficulties and burdens. One should be assured that these burdens are qualifying him and training him to become the eternal associate of Kṛṣṇa. The more burden and responsibility one is willing to take for Kṛṣṇa, the more dear he becomes to the Lord.

In the previous essay, I gave the example of how I once faltered in understanding how anything undertaken for Kṛṣṇa, including the purchase of a building, is spiritual. A year after that event, I made the same mistake, but was again corrected by Prabhupāda. That mistake was in equating spiritual advancement with retirement from practical duties. In 1972, I felt a new lift in spiritual life when Śrīla Prabhupāda awarded me *sannyāsa,* the renounced order of life. I began a busy tour of traveling and preaching in colleges and in ISKCON temples throughout the United States. But I still had a lurking misconception about spiritual life. In an inspired letter to Śrīla Prabhupāda, I mentioned that as a *sannyāsī,* I was constantly preaching and was no longer as concerned with lesser affairs such as managing the Dallas temple's incense business. In reply, Śrīla Prabhupāda corrected me:

> You mentioned that you are no longer much occupied with seeing that the rent and mortgage are paid and that the incense is sold, but G.B.C. means to be occupied with everything in the zone. It is not that now we are preachers and we can neglect all other points. No, the G.B.C. member is supposed to know everything and anything about the condition and situation of all matters within his jurisdiction. That is the meaning of secretary.

> So because we are engaged in many fields of activity I am especially relying on that knowledge of my G.B.C. assistants and secretaries to manage everything properly. But if we do not take time to understand how the financial matters are going on, then at any moment we may experience some calamity due to our inattention to these matters. Therefore you should try to keep yourself always informed how the financial matters are improving and keep your watchful eye on every feature of our Kṛṣṇa consciousness activity. That is also part of preaching work. I am also preaching daily. But I am at the same time managing everything, seeing the statements of accounts, going to the bank, giving advice on every topic, like that. Just now I have purchased one apartment house with seven apartments just adjacent to the L.A. temple and very soon we shall invest in similar properties. So practically there is no question of my neglecting the financial matters of the society, and similarly, you shall do as I am doing. That is your real business.
>
> (Letter of July 1, 1972)

Thus the real test of advancement, or liberation, is whether one is willing to give up all personal considerations to take on only that which is pleasing to the Supreme Lord. The classical example of a devotee who gave up his own personal considerations is Arjuna, on the battlefield of Kurukṣetra. At first Arjuna had his own concept of spiritual life, by which he wanted to neglect his duty of fighting and become a renounced mendicant. But Lord Kṛṣṇa wanted Arjuna to fight. When Arjuna was finally convinced, he not only took up his duty, but did so with complete surrender and willingness, despite the fact that his duty was to risk his life in an enormous battle.

This surrendered spirit is expressed in the song *Śaraṇāgati,* by Bhaktivinoda Ṭhākura: "Troubles encountered in Your service shall be the cause of great happiness, for in Your devotional service, joy and sorrow are equally great riches. Both destroy the misery of ignorance." Expressing the pure surrender of Kṛṣṇa's topmost devotees, the *gopīs*, Lord Caitanya prayed as follows: "I do not mind my personal distress. I only wish for the happiness of Kṛṣṇa, for His happiness is the goal of my life. However, if He feels great happiness in giving me distress, the distress is the best of my happiness." In his purport to this verse, Śrīla Prabhupāda speaks of the difference between un alloyed devotional service and devotional service which is covered by fruitive desire:

> Śrīla Bhaktisiddhānta Sarasvatī Ṭhākura says that a devotee does not care about his own happiness and distress; he's simply interested in seeing that Kṛṣṇa is happy, and for that purpose he engages in various activities. A pure devotee has no way of sensing happiness except by seeing that Kṛṣṇa is happy in every respect. If Kṛṣṇa becomes happy by giving him distress, such a devotee accepts that unhappiness as the greatest of all happiness. Those who are materialistic, however, who are very proud of material wealth and have no spiritual knowledge, like the *prākṛta-sahajiyās*, regard their own happiness as the aim of life. Some of them aspire to enjoy themselves by sharing the happiness of Kṛṣṇa. This is the mentality of fruitive workers who want to enjoy sense gratification by making a show of service to Kṛṣṇa.

But when a devotee acts only on behalf of Lord Kṛṣṇa for His pleasure, accepting as Kṛṣṇa's mercy whatever difficulty he may encounter in prosecuting his Kṛṣṇa conscious duties in this world, that devotee is factually situated on the liberated platform even while in this world, and the final reward for his selfless service will be the eternal, loving association of the Lord in His spiritual world.

VIII

In Praise of Śrīmad-Bhāgavatam

dharmaḥ projjhita-kaitavo 'tra paramo nirmatsarāṇāṁ satāṁ
vedyaṁ vāstavam atra vastu śivadaṁ tāpa-trayonmūlanam
śrīmad-bhāgavate mahā-muni-kṛte kiṁ vā parair īśvaraḥ
sadyo hṛdy avarudhyate 'tra kṛtibhiḥ śuśrūṣubhis tat-kṣaṇāt

"Completely rejecting all religious activities which are materially motivated, this *Bhāgavata Purāṇa* propounds the highest truth, which is understandable by those devotees who are fully pure in heart. The highest truth is reality distinguished from illusion for the welfare of all. Such truth uproots the threefold miseries. This beautiful *Bhāgavatam*, compiled by the great sage Vyāsadeva (in his maturity), is sufficient in itself for God realization. What is the need of any other scripture? As soon as one attentively and submissively hears the message of *Bhāgavatam*, by this culture of knowledge the Supreme Lord is established within his heart."

(*Bhāg*. 1.1.2)

I find a special pleasure in those verses which praise the *Bhāgavatam*. Such verses, often marking a pause in the philosophical narration, are usually clear and simple to understand, and yet they are always composed in beautiful language (*uttama-śloka*). One has to be a complete stone not to understand, at least to some degree, that the book one is reading is rare, potent literature. Since the sages give *Śrīmad-Bhāgavatam* a unique place in their praises, we should also try to appreciate it in that way. We should desire to include ourselves as hearers among the sages at Naimiṣāraṇya, or as humble additions to the audience of Śukadeva Gosvāmī's recitation to Mahārāja Parīkṣit as they sat on the bank of the Yamunā during the last seven days of Parīkṣit's life:

> That very *Śrīmad-Bhāgavatam* I shall recite before you because you are the most sincere devotee of Lord Kṛṣṇa. One who gives full attention and respect to hearing the *Śrīmad-Bhāgavatam* achieves unflinching faith in the Supreme Lord, the giver of salvation.
>
> (*Bhāg*. 2.1.10)

He who cannot at least yearn to qualify for hearing and receiving the benefit described here—attainment of love of God—is already dead, although he may still be breathing.

Today, we are receiving *Śrīmad-Bhāgavatam* from Śrīla Prabhupāda, the representative of Vyāsa. Before him, it remained hidden. As a motto to his first published volume of *Śrīmad-Bhāgavatam*, Śrīla Prabhupāda writes the following: "We know that the foreign invaders of India could break down some of the monumental architectural works in India, but they were unable to break up the perfect ideals of human civilization so far kept hidden within the Sanskrit language of Vedic wisdom."

As Śrīla Vyāsadeva had a vision of Lord Kṛṣṇa, and as he had received direct instructions from his spiritual master, Nārada Muni, to compile this *Śrīmad-Bhāgavatam*, so Śrīla Prabhupāda had his vision, and he also received instructions from his spiritual master, Bhaktisiddhānta Sarasvatī. Śrīla Prabhupāda envisioned distributing en masse the book of Śrīla Vyāsadeva. Prabhupāda did not only translate *Śrīmad-Bhāgavatam* into English, but he took it personally to the West, presented it there, and taught the people through the book and in person how to develop pure love of God.

The fact that Śrīla Prabhupāda gave *Śrīmad-Bhāgavatam* the greatest importance by dedicating his life to translating and distributing it is itself major evidence that *Śrīmad-Bhāg-*

avatam is the main scripture for all ages and all persons and places. Once he began composing his translations and commentaries in Vṛndāvana in 1959, he never ceased. For eleven straight years, while traveling all over the world spreading Kṛṣṇa consciousness, Prabhupāda always managed to rise at about one o'clock in the morning and write his Bhaktivedanta purports to the *Śrīmad-Bhāgavatam*. As part of his regular daily schedule, he would then take a morning walk, during which time his speech overflowed with verses and talks based on the *Bhāgavatam*. Then he would hold a class in the temple room, induce his disciples to chant the *Bhāgavatam śloka* along with him, and then lecture on the *Bhāgavatam* for an hour. And he would follow this schedule every day without fail. Even after returning to Vṛndāvana just before passing away from this world, when he could hardly find strength even to speak, Prabhupāda dictated the purports to the Tenth Canto.

Is not Śrīla Prabhupāda's life itself one long, eloquent praise of *Śrīmad-Bhāgavatam*? Who can fail to respond to Prabhupāda's life testimony on behalf of *Śrīmad-Bhāgavatam*? Who cannot try to read the books that Prabhupāda so lovingly and tirelessly produced? Only one who is a killer of the soul, only one who is not a human but a beast, will be uninterested in Prabhupāda's presentation of *Śrīmad-Bhāgavatam*.

These verses in the *Bhāgavatam* or elsewhere which praise the standard of *Śrīmad-Bhāgavatam* are not cheap praises. Rather, Kṛṣṇa Himself intends that *Śrīmad-Bhāgavatam* become the shelter for all souls in the Kali-yuga:

> This *Bhāgavata Purāṇa* is as brilliant as the sun, and it has arisen just after the departure of Lord Kṛṣṇa to His own abode, accompanied by religion, knowledge, and so on. Persons who have lost their vision due to the dense darkness of ignorance in the Age of Kali shall get light from this *Purāṇa*.
>
> (*Bhāg*. 1.3.43)

In commenting on this verse Śrīla Prabhupāda writes, "One who can see *Śrīmad-Bhāgavatam* can see also Lord Kṛṣṇa in person. They are identical."

Aside from the recommendations of *Śrīmad-Bhāgavatam* by sages and saints, *Śrīmad-Bhāgavatam* is self-evidently of the highest quality. It rejects all materially motivated forms of religion and gives only pure devotional service, culminating in the pastimes of Lord Kṛṣṇa as given in the Tenth Canto, which is the essence of *Śrīmad-Bhāgavatam*. If a reader gradually studies *Śrīmad-Bhāgavatam* and develops his understanding and appreciation of it through the first nine cantos, then he will be qualified to hear the transcendental activities of the Personality of Godhead as directly presented in the Tenth Canto.

The evidence is overwhelmingly in favor of our study and appreciation of the spotless *Purāṇa*. And the verses of the *Bhāgavatam* which praise *Śrīmad-Bhāgavatam* itself are especially uplifting. They convince and inspire us in a most direct way. They are not a digression from the topics discussed in the *Bhāgavatam*, but they focus on the center of the whole process:

> O greatly fortunate Śukadeva Gosvāmī, please continue narrating *Śrīmad-Bhāgavatam* so that I can place my mind upon the Supreme Soul Lord Kṛṣṇa, and, being completely freed from material qualities, thus relinquish this body.
>
> Persons who hear *Śrīmad-Bhāgavatam* regularly and are always taking the matter very seriously will have the Personality of Godhead Śrī Kṛṣṇa manifested in their hearts within a short time.
>
> (*Bhāg*. 2.8.3–4)

As a fallen, inattentive rascal, I nevertheless adjure myself and my readers: Let us not wait until tomorrow. Let us read *Śrīmad-Bhāgavatam* today and every day, and let us learn to join sincerely in the praises of Śrī Kṛṣṇa's beautiful book.

IX
The Boston Brāhmaṇas

yathā kāñcanatāṁ yāti
kāṁsyaṁ rasa-vidhānataḥ
tathā dīkṣā-vidhānena
dvijatvaṁ jāyate nṛṇām

"As bell metal is turned to gold when mixed with mercury in an alchemical process, so one who is properly trained and initiated by a bona fide spiritual master immediately becomes a *brāhmaṇa*."

(*Hari-bhakti-vilāsa*, quoted in Cc. *Mādhya* 15.108)

It was a great, historical event: the first brahminical initiation to be held in the International Society for Krishna Consciousness. The date: May 1968. The place: a humble, one-room storefront which was the temple and headquarters of ISKCON Boston. Śrīla Prabhupāda's sudden announcement that he would hold second initiations for his first-initiated disciples came as a complete surprise to all of us. Almost fifteen years later it still seems startling, and many people continue to question us about it. How can Westerners become *brāhmaṇas*? What is a *brāhmaṇa*, anyway? Can Westerners be considered bona fide *brāhmaṇas* by the *brāhmaṇas* of India? These and similar questions are all answered by this verse composed five hundred years ago by Sanātana Gosvāmī in *Hari-bhakti-vilāsa*.

That first *brāhmaṇa* initiation in Boston was for men

only. Pradyumna dāsa, Gaurasundara dāsa, and I sat wearing our *dhotīs*, but bare chested, around a crudely arranged fire *yajña* in the small storefront. There were no more than twenty onlookers, including the women devotees, guests of the temple, and Mr. Matthews, a specially invited guest from Harvard University who was a graduate student in Hindu and Sanskrit studies. But because everything had happened so suddenly, none of the devotees from either the New York or Montreal temples, the two nearest ISKCON centers, were in attendance. I personally felt very proud that such an important, first-time event was occurring as a "Boston-only" exclusive, and I imagined how Brahmānanda and the other New York devotees must have been envying our fledgling center.

Śrīla Prabhupāda required that a devotee be initiated by *hari-nāma* initiation for one year in order to receive second initiation. That meant we each had to be strictly observing the four prohibitions and chanting sixteen rounds, and Prabhupāda had to accept us as a reliable devotee. We knew, of course, that there was a difference between those who claimed to be *brāhmaṇas* by birth, as in the caste system of India, and the bona fide *brāhmaṇas* like Nārada Muni and other who were great Vaiṣṇavas. In the *varṇāśrama* system the *brāhmaṇa* is the highest social order, and he is responsible for practicing and disseminating Kṛṣṇa consciousness. One who is fixed in Kṛṣṇa consciousness and serving under the order of the bona fide spiritual master is already better than a *brāhmaṇa*. These things we had already heard from Śrīla Prabhupāda. We were also aware that basically we knew nothing and had no qualifications, and yet if Śrīla Prabhupāda wanted to initiate us as *brahmacārīs*, as *gṛhasthas*, as first initiates or second initiates—or whatever — his decision was absolute and in tune with the will of Kṛṣṇa.

When Prabhupāda had first arrived in Boston, we had jokingly told him of the phrase "Boston *brāhmaṇas*," a nineteenth-century phrase describing the intellectual aristocracy which dominated Boston at that time. Oliver Wendel Holmes, who first used the term, apparently had at least a faint idea that a *brāhmaṇa* was a highly qualified person. But we had never dreamed that Prabhupāda would make us real *brāhmaṇas.* When Prabhupāda had first mentioned it in a casual way while in his room a few blocks away from our storefront, the devotees had immediately asked Prabhupāda what it all meant. Śrīla Prabhupāda had deferred an explanation and had said that he would explain it sufficiently when he actually held the *brāhmaṇa* initiation. So even at the time of sitting down before the fire *yajña,* we had little specific idea of what it meant. We had heard that we would receive a *mantra* and that Prabhupāda was preparing some threads to put on our bodies. We were also appreciating the thrill of ever-new experiences which characterized life with Śrīla Prabhupāda in Kṛṣṇa consciousness.

In his lecture Prabhupāda explained that his spiritual master, Śrīla Bhaktisiddhānta Sarasvatī Ṭhākura, had introduced brahminical initiation for disciples not born of *brāhmaṇa* families. He said that the Vedic scriptures offered much evidence that by associating with pure devotees, anyone could become a *brāhmaṇa.* In fact, the scriptures said that if one born in a *brāhmaṇa* family did not behave as a *brāhmaṇa,* then he should not be accepted as a *brāhmaṇa.* So it was in following Śrīla Bhaktisiddhānta Sarasvatī and the Vedic scriptures that Prabhupāda was now going to give brahminical initiation to his disciples.

After Śrīla Prabhupāda finished his discourse, he invited his new academic acquaintance from Harvard, Mr. Matthews, if he had any relevant questions. Mr. Matthews asked about the importance of the Gāyatrī *mantra* and whether the devotees would take on any new fasting vows. Śrīla Prabhupāda replied that the Hare Kṛṣṇa *mantra* was itself sufficient for delivering the disciple back to Godhead, but the Gāyatrī *mantra* would increase one's Kṛṣṇa consciousness. As for new vows of fasting, Prabhupāda said that that was not necessary, since the eating of Kṛṣṇa *prasādam* was already sanctified.

Śrīla Prabhupāda asked us to come forward one at a time and sit beside him. When my turn came, I sat beside Śrīla Prabḥupāda, and he handed me a piece of paper on which was typed the words of the Gāyatrī *mantra.* He then recited each word into my right ear, and he showed me how to count on my fingers. He then placed the *brāhmaṇa* thread over my shoulder and body. At this time the other devotees in attendance were chanting Hare Kṛṣṇa in *kīrtana.* The accumulated noise made it somewhat difficult to hear Prabhupāda, and I had to bend close to him. He then gave me another piece of paper, on which was written the *yathā kāñcanatāṁ yāti* verse of Sanātana Gosvāmī. Prabhupāda said this could be chanted occasionally.

The next morning Prabhupāda held a second *brāhmaṇa* initiation ceremony. This was for the women, after they had made a feminist protest about being excluded. Soon after that, groups of devotees came from both New York and Montreal to also receive second initiation. Thus on several occasions we got to hear Śrīla Prabhupāda lecture about the meaning of *brāhmaṇa* and the authenticity of his awarding this status to those born in the West.

If an ISKCON *brāhmaṇa* who is not born in a *brāhmaṇa*-Hindu family is challenged as to whether he is actually a *brāhmaṇa,* this verse by Sanātana Gosvāmī serves as a passport or official documentation. The analogy in Sanātana Gosvāmī's verse is directly applicable to Westerners. By their birth and upbringing they are considered *mlecchas,* or those whose behavior is abominable when judged by the standards of Vedic culture. Westerners are normally meat-eaters, usually engage in illicit sex of one form or another, and are usually addicted to alcohol or other intoxicating drugs. Therefore, in their normal Western mood, they could never be considered *brāhmaṇas*. It is also stated in the *Vedas* that unless one is a *brāhmaṇa* he is not fit to study the Vedic literature. If one is contaminated in his body, mind, and speech, then he cannot understand the teachings of the *Bhagavad-gītā,* nor should such a person be allowed to perform brahminical functions in the temple, such as cooking, or bathing and dressing the Deities. Neither can such a person speak in an authoritative way about the science of Kṛṣṇa consciousness. But it does not follow that one born and raised as a *mleccha* is unable to change his situation in this lifetime. Just as base metal can be changed to gold by the proper mixture, so by associating with a pure devotee a *mleccha* can turn into a Vaiṣṇava. The factual basis of this is that everyone is pure spirit soul, and when one comes to the human form of life, then Kṛṣṇa consciousness is possible if one takes properly to the *bhakti-yoga* process.

If we consider this verse in *Hari-bhakti-vilāsa* to be an important form of spiritual ID, like a passport, then there are many other verses which can be put forward as further documentary proofs, as long as they are presented by a sincere, practicing devotee who works under the guidance of a bona fide spiritual master. One of these verses occurs in the Second Canto of the *Śrīmad-Bhāgavatam:*

kirāta-hūṇāndhra-pulinda-pulkaśā
ābhīra-śumbhā yavanāḥ khasādayaḥ
ye 'nye ca pāpā yad-apāśrayāśrayāḥ
śudhyanti tasmai prabhaviṣṇave namaḥ

Kirāta, Hūṇa, Āndhra, Pulinda, Pulkaśa, Ābhīra, Śumbha, Yavana, and the Khasa races and even others who are addicted to sinful acts can be purified by taking shelter of the devotees of the Lord due to His being the supreme power. I beg to offer my respectful obeisances unto Him.

(*Bhāg*. 2.4.18)

This verse is important because it specifically mentions different races and nationalities spread around the globe, including Mid-Eastern nations, the continent of Africa, and European denominations as well. The practice of *bhakti-yoga* is so pure that any one of these human groups, some of whom are considered to be almost savages or tribe people, can rise all the way up to the standard of a Goswami or a pure devotee.

I once quoted this *kirāta-hūṇāndhra* verse before an assembly in the courtyard of the ancient Rādhā-Dāmodara temple in Vṛndāvana, India. While passing through the temple courtyard, the caste *gosvāmī* in charge of the temple heard me recite this verse from memory. He was familiar with this *śloka,* and upon hearing it he stopped, raised his eyebrows significantly, and smiled. Even if in his heart he could not accept the truth that we ISKCON devotees from the West were also *brāhmaṇas* and *gosvāmīs,* nevertheless, he could not deny the actual purport of the verse, and it pleased him to hear it from the lips of a white man.

Among the verses that I have heard Śrīla Prabhupāda quote in defense of Western *brāhmaṇas,* the one which I have noted him use more than any other is a statement spoken by Nārada Muni to Mahārāja Yudhiṣṭhira:

yasya yal lakṣaṇaṁ proktaṁ
puṁso varṇābhivyañjakam
yad anyatrāpi dṛśyeta
tat tenaiva vinirdiśet

If one shows the symptoms of being a *brāhmaṇa, kṣatriya, vaiśya,* or *śūdra,* as described above, even if he has appeared in a different class, he should be accepted according to those symptoms of classification."

(*Bhāg.* 7.11.35)

This verse is irrefutable, not only because it is stated in the *śāstra,* but also because of its logical sense. In former ages, if one were born of a *brāhmaṇa* mother and father, one would usually be trained according to the brahminical standard. But in Kali-yuga, the first *saṁskāra*, known as *Garbhādhāna-saṁskāra*, where the conception of the child is performed as part of a religious ceremony, is not observed. Other *saṁskāras* are also not observed, so in this age no one can be considered a *brāhmaṇa* by birth. The scriptures also state, *kalau śūdra-sambhavaḥ:* "In the age of Kali everyone is born a fourth-class person, or *śudra*." How can one be considered a true *brāhmaṇa* if he is unaware of the Supreme Truth, smokes and drinks, or works at a non-brahminical occupation? And why should a person, regardless of his birth, be denied elevation in spiritual life up to the status of *brāhmaṇa*, provided he is properly trained and guided? Only a perverted interpretation of the *varṇāśrama* system can bring about a conclusion that one born in a lower birth must stay in a lower status. Lord Kṛṣṇa Himself, who is the original creator of the *varṇāśrama*, states, *guṇa-karma-vibhāgaśaḥ*, which means that the division of four social and four spiritual orders is determined by work and quality, not by birth.

Another wonderful "document" verse about elevation to brahminical status is spoken by Lord Kapiladeva to His mother, Devahūti, in the Third Canto of *Śrīmad-Bhāgavatam:*

yan-nāmadheya-śravaṇānukīrtanād
yat-prahvaṇād yat-smaraṇād api kvacit
śvādo 'pi sadyaḥ savanāya kalpate
kutaḥ punas te bhagavan nu darśanāt

aho bata śva-paco 'to garīyān
yaj-jihvāgre vartate nāma tubhyam
tepus tapas te juhuvuḥ sasnur āryā
brahmānūcur nāma gṛṇanti ye te

To say nothing of the spiritual advancement of persons who see the Supreme Person face to face, even a person born in a family of dog-eaters immediately becomes eligible to perform Vedic sacrifices if he once utters the holy name of the Su-

> preme Personality of Godhead or chants about Him, hears about His pastimes, offers Him obeisances, or even remembers Him.
>
> Oh, how glorious are they whose tongues are chanting Your holy name! Even if born in the families of dog-eaters, such persons are worshipable. Persons who chant the holy name of Your Lordship must have excuted all kinds of austerities and fire sacrifices and achieved all the good manners of the *Āryans.* To be chanting the holy name of Your Lordship, they must have bathed at holy places of pilgrimage, studied the *Vedas,* and fulfilled everything required.
>
> (*Bhāg.* 3.33.6–7)

Lord Kapila's statements awaken us once again to the unrivaled potency of the holy name of God, as in the Hare Kṛṣṇa *mantra.* No matter how fallen or sinful one may appear to be, if he is fortunate enough to chant the holy name, then he becomes topmost among men.

A man in India once said to me, "Yes, you devotees can become equal to or even better than *brāhmaṇas* in this lifetime—but you cannot become *brāhmaṇas* in this lifetime." But in these verses Lord Kapila states that the chanter of Hare Kṛṣṇa is eligible to perform the Vedic sacrifices, which are the special province of the *brāhmaṇas.* Previously quoted verses also attest to the fact that the devotee in Kṛṣṇa consciousness can engage in the occupational duties of a *brāhmaṇa.*

Foolish people may always criticize, but if one has the support of *guru, śāstra,* and *sādhu,* he should be confident and not be disappointed in his brahminical work. Prabhupāda himself was challenged by caste *brāhmaṇas* who claimed that Prabhupāda was ruining Hinduism by his acceptance of *mlecchas* as *brāhmaṇas.* But Śrīla Prabhupāda was confident that he was following the sastric injunctions of Nārada Muni, Lord Kapila, Lord Caitanya, and Lord Kṛṣṇa. Most Hindu institutions in India have come to warmly accept and commend ISKCON, and as for his critics, Prabhupāda sometimes remarked, "Who cares for them?"

Our real concern should be never to disgrace our spiritual master by falling from the standard of *brāhmaṇa* as defined in the Kṛṣṇa consciousness movement. All concession has been made and all risk taken by Śrīla Prabhupāda to bring us to the brahminical standard. If we fall, then it is the worst ungratefulness. In attending to brahminical details, the Western devotees, at least those of the present generation, may be open to committing certain discrepancies. But as long as we do not neglect the main activity of regularly chanting Hare Kṛṣṇa, strictly avoiding the four sinful activities, and fully engaging our energies in authorized preaching work, then the criticisms are mistaken. Forms of service and worship of Lord Kṛṣṇa may differ slightly in various parts of the world. This is accounted for in the instructions of Nārada Muni to Dhruva Mahārāja. Nārada told Dhruva to follow the rules and regulations, but since Dhruva Mahārāja was worshiping in the forest, Nārada added, "This should be done in consideration of place, time, and attendant conveniences and inconveniences." These criticisms of devotees of ISKCON can always be countered by sastric references. But if devotees fall down in their strict following of regulative principles, or if we give up the preaching work, then certainly our *mleccha* births and upbringing will be recalled again, and we will be rightly condemned. We should follow Śrīla Prabhupāda's advice which he gave on a morning walk in Boston in 1968, after seeing a group of his newly initiated *brāhmaṇas.* "Here come the *brāhmaṇas,*" said Prabhupāda. "But now don't be *brāhmaṇas* in name only."

X

Tridaṇḍi Sannyāsa

etāṁ sa āsthāya parātma-niṣṭhām
adhyāsitāṁ pūrvatamair mahadbhiḥ
ahaṁ tariṣyāmi duranta-pāraṁ
tamo mukundāṅghri-niṣevayaiva

"I shall cross over the insurmountable ocean of nescience by being firmly fixed in the service of the lotus feet of Kṛṣṇa. This was approved by the previous *ācāryas,* who were fixed in firm devotion to the Lord, Paramātmā, the Supreme Personality of Godhead."

Śrīla Prabhupāda handed me this verse on a piece of paper as part of the ceremony when I received *sannyāsa* initiation. The paper also contained a purport by Śrīla Prabhupāda which described the history of the *sannyāsa* order in Vaiṣṇavism. The purport proved that *sannyāsa* was not the monopoly of the philosophical impersonalists led by Śaṅkarācārya. The purport also described that the Vaiṣṇava's *sannyāsa* rod (*daṇḍa*) held four rods, signifying that the spirit soul is engaged with his body, mind, and words in the service of Kṛṣṇa. But the main point of the verse and purport was that a Vaiṣṇava *sannyāsī* is meant for dedicating his life completely to the service of Mukunda, Lord Kṛṣṇa. By way of explaining this verse, I would like to recall some events surrounding my own initiation into *sannyāsa,* and some of the instructions I received from Śrīla Prabhupāda.

Śrīla Prabhupāda knew that most disciples would belong to the *gṛhastha āśrama* (married life), but he said there cannot be a preaching movement unless there are *sannyāsī* devotees traveling around the world. For the purpose of preaching, Lord Caitanya Himself took *sannyāsa* at an early age, and Śrīla Prabhupāda also wanted to initiate young *sannyāsīs*. Prabhupāda saw the world as in a critical condition due to lack of Kṛṣṇa consciousness, and to increase the preaching in this time of emergency, he initiated promising young men into the austere stage of renounced life, where one has to be free of all sexual relationships and totally dedicated to service to Kṛṣṇa. That is the way of Kṛṣṇa consciousness — first one takes a position of service, and then one attains the qualifications for the post.

In the material world, to be a judge you must first become an undergraduate student, then a postgraduate, then enter law school, pass the bar exam, and become a lawyer. Only then can you be appointed to the position of judge. But in Kṛṣṇa consciousness it is different. As Prabhupāda used to say, *first* one sits on the bench of the high court judge, and *then* he attains the qualifications. This reminds me of the cowboy movies where the sheriff would appoint deputies. There would be an emergency chase after some outlaws, and the sheriff would put badges on whoever was willing to join the posse and chase after them. Kali-yuga is a real emergency, and many *sannyāsīs* are required to join the worldwide posse to capture outlaw souls for Lord Caitanya by "shooting" them with the holy name.

The message of Kṛṣṇa consciousness is so simple to understand that even a little child can repeat it if he has the faith and the conviction that Kṛṣṇa is the Supreme Personality of Godhead and that everyone should chant Hare Kṛṣṇa. And so Śrīla Prabhupāda's disciples became *sannyāsīs* despite their young age. Of course, Prabhupāda's *sannyāsī* candidates had to have already proven themselves by observing the four prohibitions against sinful life, by chanting sixteen rounds of the Hare Kṛṣṇa *mantra* daily, and by being ready to give up all connnections with women and family.

In one sense, the renounced order of *sannyāsa* is external, and preaching does not require taking *sannyāsa.* Lord Caitanya Mahāprabhu said, "It does not matter whether one is a *brāhmaṇa,* a *sannyāsī,* or a *śūdra.* If he knows the science of Kṛṣṇa, he can be a spiritual master." But because a householder's social position may sometimes inhibit his full surrender to Kṛṣṇa, *sannyāsa* gives a person more freedom to preach. And because of his factual renunciation of all paraphernalia and association of family and women, the *sannyāsī* does receive special honor and facility.

In 1972, Śrīla Prabhupāda suggested to myself and others that we come forward and request *sannyāsa.* I was a *gṛhastha* at the time, although I had not been living with my wife for over two years. I was in Dallas, Texas, pioneering with the *gurukula.* We heard through letters from Prabhupāda's secretary that Prabhupāda was not very satisfied with the leaders on his ISKCON Governing Body Commission. According to Prabhupāda's secretary, the G.B.C. men were stressing management too much and becoming attached to controlling men and money. They were not preaching enough. Śrīla Prabhupāda even sent a telegram to the G.B.C.: "Your material formulas will not help you. This movement is meant for us to become mad after Kṛṣṇa." Prabhupāda also said, "Better all the G.B.C. take *sannyāsa* and preach; they should do some substantial preaching work."

About half a dozen G.B.C. members wrote Śrīla Prabhupāda saying they would like to take *sannyāsa,* and in most cases he accepted the requests. He then began to initiate them. During this time Śrīla Prabhupāda was in India, and there he initiated Tamāl Kṛṣṇa Goswami as the first G.B.C. *sannyāsī.* Then Prabhupāda went to Japan and turned Sudāmā, his G.B.C. man there, into a *sannyāsī*. I had written Prabhupāda a letter asking for *sannyāsa,* and in his reply he agreed to this. On his invitation, four of us went to Los Angeles for our initiations.

We spent almost a week in Los Angeles in Śrīla Prabhupāda's company. Prabhupāda was lecturing on *Śrīmad-Bhāgavatam,* Second Canto, Chapter Three, entitled, "Pure Devotional Service: The Change in Heart." In that chapter, the devotee's kindness is mentioned. Śrīla Prabhupāda said, "Just like these devotees about to take *sannyāsa,* they are kind. One of them has a very nice family and wife, but for the benefit of all others, to preach he is going to give that up. So this is kindness. *Sannyāsa* means to give up all material attachment." In this way, Prabhupāda prepared us for the step we were to take.

Some of us got together and studied a purport in the *Bhagavad-gītā* (16.1) where Śrīla Prabhupāda discusses specific qualifications of a *sannyāsī*. A *sannyāsī* is supposed to be *abhayam,* fearless, ready to live alone. He must also be *śaucam,* clean and pure. In his purport, Śrīla Prabhupāda says that the most important rule for the *sannyāsī* who wishes to purify his existence is to strictly avoid intimacy with women, and he cites Lord Caitanya as an example of a *sannyāsī* who never dealt closely with His women followers. And a *sannyāsī* should have *jñāna,* knowledge of the scriptures, so he can impart knowledge to others.

Śrīla Prabhupāda very kindly held our *sannyāsa* initiation ceremony on the appearance day of Lord Nṛsiṁhadeva in May 1972. He said at that time that there would be much opposition from atheists but that Lord Nṛsiṁhadeva would protect us. "So by this *sannyāsa* you should preach," he said, and he repeated this instruction about four times for emphasis: "Preach! Preach! Preach! Preach!" Then he gave us our *daṇḍas*.

After the initiation, the four of us went into his room.

Kīrtanānanda Mahārāja was visiting from New Vrindaban. Śrīla Prabhupāda saw him standing in the back of the room and said, "Give Kīrtanānanda Mahārāja a seat." Kīrtanānanda Mahārāja said, "No, it's all right. I think if I sit down I may sleep." Prabhupāda laughed and said, "Yes. There is a kind of *sannyāsī* who always moves. He takes a vow never to stay still. If you want to talk to him, you have to walk or run beside him. He never stays still."

In his room, Prabhupāda said to the four of us, "Now you are all *sannyāsīs*."

"What exactly are our names?" we asked.

He said, "Whatever your name is, you just put 'Goswami' at the end." Then he had each of us say our name. "What is *your* name?" he would ask, and we would each say our name. "Yes," he said when it was my turn, "now you are Satsvarūpa dāsa Goswami."

In Los Angeles we had been hearing much *sannyāsa* lore. We heard that a *sannyāsī* is supposed to sleep in a certain way, keep a certain kind of underwear, and worship his *daṇḍa* by offering food to it. We took these things seriously and thought there were many intricate things that we would have to learn about *sannyāsa*. We asked Śrīla Prabhupāda if he would give us some instructions about the rules, regulations, and behavior of a *sannyāsī*. Śrīla Prabhupāda described very few details, but he did give us one main rule to follow: "Sometimes you will be in the home of a very rich man, and sometimes you will be in the home of a poor man. When you are in the home of a rich man, you may see his different paraphernalia, but you should not desire to have it. You may think, 'I once had some wealth. I could have attained this level of enjoyment if I had continued. Maybe I could try again.' That attraction may be there, but you should not have remorse. Similarly, when you see a pretty young woman, you may think, 'I once had a wife or girl friend like this. This young woman reminds me of her. Since this woman is like the previous woman I knew, maybe I could again enjoy, with this one.' But these thoughts are forbidden. You should not have any remorse over what you have done by taking *sannyāsa*." Prabhupāda thus forbade us to regret having given up wealth and the possibility of enjoying young girls. This and the order to "preach, preach, preach, preach" were the only specific instructions for *sannyāsīs* which he gave.

Śrīla Prabhupāda had us collect alms, *guru-dakṣiṇā*. Hṛdayānanda Mahārāja and I went out together in the neighborhood in Culver City, carrying our new *daṇḍas* and knocking on doors. We did not collect very much—two envelopes containing change and bills—but we personally gave our collections to Prabhupāda.

The next morning we went on a walk with Prabhupāda on Venice Beach. It was a walk only for those who had taken *sannyāsa*. We again asked Prabhupāda some of the questions about the lore we had heard. "Prabhupāda, we heard that a *sannyāsī* is supposed to keep one Deity in his mind and mentally worship that Deity while he travels." Prabhupāda was quite indifferent to the question. He said, "Lord Caitanya visited different temples, but He never carried a Deity with Him. A *sannyāsī* must always keep his *daṇḍa* and beads. The *sannyāsī* especially must chant *hari-nāma*. He has to worship with his beads."

We then asked, "Prabhupāda, we've heard that the *sannyāsa* staff, the *daṇḍa*, is like Viṣṇu. It is worshipable, and one can offer food to it." He laughed and said, "Who said that? No. The three rods stand for body, mind, and words dedicated in the service of Kṛṣṇa. The *jīva* is the fourth rod." So that rumor was cleared up.

"Do not get entangled in management," Śrīla Prabhupāda emphasized, "but travel and preach." We took that very literally at first, and all four of us went different ways. I was invited to San Francisco, and I went alone. I especially looked for different opportunities to preach to the non-devotees, but because the temple members were too busy to help me, I could not get many formal speaking engagements. In San Francisco, however, I met a devotee named Janamejaya, who wanted to take *sannyāsa* in the future. He therefore asked to be my assistant, and he offered the use of his car. So off we went on a U.S. tour.

Although I was a *sannyāsī,* Janamejaya, my assistant, enforced a rule that we should not spend any of the money we carried with us. He thought it would be a sin if we spent a dollar of this money. I thought this was foolish, yet he would not allow it. We would not even spend our money for gas; we would have to beg money at a gas station. Every time we ran out of gas, we would again pull in at a gas station and beg for the money. We would not spend money for a motel but slept in his car. For food we begged at fruit wholesalers. For some reason Kṛṣṇa sent me a servant to punish me by making me practice the *tapasya* of not spending any money.

We traveled widely, to Utah, to Colorado, down to Dallas, Mississippi, Atlanta, and then up to Detroit. When we passed by a park, we would sometimes stop and speak to the young people and ask them to chant with us. Many of them had never seen devotees, and they were often interested. The trip lasted two weeks, and then we arrived in Detroit, where Bhagavān dāsa was the president and G.B.C. At that time, I received a wonderful letter from Prabhupāda. After taking *sannyāsa,* I had written to tell him how happy I was. In his return letter he said that he had received other blissful letters from his *sannyāsīs* and that he was very pleased with them. Also in his letter, Śrīla Prabhupāda instructed me to institute a *Śrīmad-Bhāgavatam* class in each temple within my zone. He himself had just introduced the morning class in Los Angeles. Prior to this there had been no formal procedure for holding classes in the ISKCON temples. But now all devotees were to attend and chant a Sanskrit *śloka* together; a senior devotee would then lecture for forty-five minutes. In his letter Śrīla Prabhupāda indicated that as a *sannyāsī* and a G.B.C. member, I had an important duty to help him institute the *Bhāgavatam* class. He said there are many thousands of verses in the *Śrīmad-Bhāgavatam,* and each day we should speak on one verse. He promised we would see "new lights" in the verses.

I had written Śrīla Prabhupāda about my traveling. In reply he stated that it was more important for me to preach to the devotees than to the nondevotees. He said that we want to boil the milk so that we have some good-quality devotees. In my letter to him I had also expressed that I did not feel I was a very bold preacher. His reply was encouraging:

> You mentioned that you are not yet a very bold preacher, but you will become bold if you have got sincerity. In the beginning also I could not speak. But Kṛṣṇa is within you, and when you are serving Him sincerely He will give you courage, boldness, everything. We are not going to bluff anyone or cheat others, and we are delivering the message on behalf of the Supreme Lord, so we haven't got anything to fear and we should be always mindful of our topmost position of occupation of life.
>
> (Letter of June 16, 1972)

With Janamejaya I traveled to the temples in my zone, conducted classes for the devotees, and learned the Sanskrit pronunciation. I would also go downtown every day for public *hari-nāma* and book distribution.

I wrote another letter to Prabhupāda, in which I again told him how happy and free I was now that I was a *sannyāsī.* I mentioned in the letter that when I used to be the president of ISKCON Dallas I was very concerned with the incense business and raising money to keep the *gurukula* going, but now I was just preaching. This was my understanding of my duties as a *sannyāsī.* But Śrīla Prabhupāda wrote me another letter stating that I should remain concerned with finances and all matters of management. He clarified that my *sannyāsa* role was not just to be footloose and travel here and there in a carefree manner.

Later that summer I personally met again with Śrīla Prabhupāda, and he encouraged me to obtain a bus and hold festivals as I traveled. Śrīla Prabhupāda's instructions for *sannyāsa* were not stereotyped or limited to only a single aspect of preaching; "Kṛṣṇa's head is important," he said, "and so is His foot."

My Godbrother Tamāl Kṛṣṇa Goswami recalls how at his own initiation into *sannyāsa,* Śrīla Prabhupāda repeatedly uttered the *sannyāsa* verse of the *Śrīmad-Bhāgavatam,* beginning with the line *etāṁ sa āsthāya parātma niṣṭhām.* By Śrīla Prabhupāda's emphasis, Tamāl Kṛṣṇa entered more into the meaning of *sannyāsa,* as expressed thousands of years ago by a *brāhmaṇa* from Avantī *deśa.* Even after the initiation,Śrīla Prabhupāda continued to recite the verse in the presence of his disciples while traveling in a car or instructing Tamāl Kṛṣṇa Goswami in his duties of traveling and preaching.

There are other sections in the Vaiṣṇava literature which also inspire one's feelings for the life of *sannyāsa.* Lord Caitanya's *sannyāsa* adventures, as He traveled for six years in South India, are especially noteworthy. Kṛṣṇadāsa Kavirāja describes that Lord Caitanya was very eager to be free for practicing the austerities of traveling and preaching. When Lord Caitanya finally broke away from the loving association of His many friends and followers who had detained Him in Navadvīpa and Jagannātha Purī, He walked along the road in *sannyāsa* ecstasy, accompanied by one servant. In a mood of complete surrender, He sang a Vedic verse, calling out for the mercy and protection of Kṛṣṇa:

Kṛṣṇa! Kṛṣṇa! Kṛṣṇa! Kṛṣṇa!
Kṛṣṇa! Kṛṣṇa! Kṛṣṇa! he!
Kṛṣṇa! Kṛṣṇa! Kṛṣṇa! Kṛṣṇa!
Kṛṣṇa! Kṛṣṇa! Kṛṣṇa! he!
Kṛṣṇa! Kṛṣṇa! Kṛṣṇa! Kṛṣṇa!
Kṛṣṇa! Kṛṣṇa! rakṣa mām!
Kṛṣṇa! Kṛṣṇa! Kṛṣṇa! Kṛṣṇa!
Kṛṣṇa! Kṛṣṇa! pāhi mām!
Rāma! Rāghava! Rāma! Rāghava!
Rāma! Rāghava! rakṣa mām!
Kṛṣṇa! Keśava! Kṛṣṇa! Keśava!
Kṛṣṇa! Keśava! pāhi mām!

(Cc. *Madhya* 7.96)

Another favorite narration of mine relevant to *sannyāsa* is in the *Caitanya-caritāmṛta,* wherein Sanātana Gosvāmī renounces his government post to join Lord Caitanya. Sanātana was put into jail by the Muhammadan ruler, but he finally escaped. He also escaped a dangerous situation in a hotel where he was almost murdered for his money. Finally free of all encumbrances after renouncing his servant Īśāna, Sanātana Gosvāmī traveled bereft of material goods but in high transcendental spirits. In the mood of a new *sannyāsī,* he went to join Lord Caitanya.

Nārada Muni's abrupt initiation into *sannyāsa* life, starting at the age of five with the death of his mother, is one of the most poignant autobiographical accounts within the *Śrīmad-Bhāgavatam.* Nārada was fortunate to hear about Kṛṣṇa from great devotees who visited his mother's house, and after the death of his mother, the young boy set out alone to practice Kṛṣṇa consciousness as he had seen and heard it from the *bhaktivedantas.* Commenting on Nārada's youthful travels, Śrīla Prabhupāda writes, "It is the duty of a mendicant to have experience of all varieties of God's creation as *parivrājakācārya,* or traveling alone through all forests, hills, towns, villages, etc., to gain faith in God and strength of mind as well as to enlighten the inhabitants to the message of God. A *sannyāsī* is duty-bound to take all these risks without any fear, and the most typical *sannyāsī* of the present age is Lord Caitanya."

Śrīla Prabhupāda's modern-day *sannyāsa* adventures as "jet-age *parivrājakācārya*" are forever an emblem of the fullest realization of *sannyāsa*. After receiving his *sannyāsa* initiation in 1959, Śrīla Prabhupāda absorbed himself in writing and producing the first volume of *Śrīmad-Bhāgavatam*. He was aware that his intense endeavors to print his book in New Delhi may have seemed at odds with the typical behavior of a *sannyāsī* who stays at a holy place chanting on his beads. Śrīla Prabhupāda explained himself in his Preface to the *Śrīmad-Bhāgavatam*:

> The path of fruitive activities, the path of earn money and enjoy life, as is going on generally, appears to have become also our profession although we have renounced the order of worldly life! They see that we are moving in the cities, in the government offices, banks and other business places for promoting the publication of *Shrimad-Bhagavatam*. They also see that we are moving in the press, paper market and amongst the bookbinders also away from our residence at Vrindaban, and thus they conclude sometimes mistakenly that we are also doing the same business in the dress of a mendicant!
>
> Even though we are not in the Himalayas, even though we talk of business, even though we deal in rupees and paises, still, simply because we are one hundred percent servants of the Lord and are engaged in the service of broadcasting the message of His glories, certainly we shall transcend and get through the invincible impasse of *maya* and reach the effulgent kingdom of God to render Him face to face eternal service, in full bliss and knowledge. We are confident of this factual position and we may also assure our numerous readers that they will also achieve the same result simply by hearing the glories of the Lord.

Śrīla Prabhupāda continued this standard of constant

travel on a worldwide scale, and even when his movement became a multi million-dollar enterprise he remained as humble, as renounced, and in the same high, transcendental spirits as the great mendicant-wanderers of ancient Vedic days.

Now, with the publication of the Eleventh Canto of *Śrīmad-Bhāgavatam* with translation and commentary by Śrīla Hridayānanda dāsa Goswami Ācāryadeva and Gopī parāṇadhana dāsa, we have the *paramparā* presentation of the *sannyāsa* verse spoken by the Avantī *brāhmaṇa* within the context of the complete *Bhāgavatam* narration. The "Song of the Avantī Brāhmaṇa" is itself a wonderful testimony to the qualities of *sannyāsa*. The verse climaxes a number of verses in which the Avantī *brāhmaṇa* expresses his complete dependence on and surrender to Lord Kṛṣṇa, even when faced with the severe difficulties that occur for a renounced person. While trying to pursue his *sannyāsa* practices, the Avantī *brāhmaṇa* was particularly harassed by materialists. But he accepted this as a reaction to his previous sins, and he always meditated on Kṛṣṇa and desired only to serve Him.

From these sastric descriptions and personal examples of devotees' lives, we can understand that Kṛṣṇa and the pure devotees are very pleased with any soul who gives up his false claims for enjoyment within this world and takes to the path of renunciation as chalked out by previous spiritual masters. Only when one becomes disgusted with attempts to enjoy materialistic family life and with its concentration on sex pleasure and the accumulation of worldly goods and prestige can one hope to cross over the ocean of nescience, the cycle of repeated birth and death. The method for successful detachment and freedom from suffering is described in essence by this *sannyāsa* verse from *Śrīmad-Bhāgavatam*: "I shall cross over the insurmountable ocean of nescience by being firmly fixed in the service of the lotus feet of Kṛṣṇa. This was approved by the previous *ācāryas*, who are fixed in firm devotion to the Lord, Paramātmā, the Supreme Personality of Godhead."

XI
Great Hope

nāmnām akāri bahudhā nija-sarva-śaktis
tatrārpitā niyamitaḥ smaraṇe na kālaḥ
etādṛśī tava kṛpā bhagavan mamāpi
durdaivam īdṛśam ihājani nānurāgaḥ

"O my Lord, Your holy name alone can render all benediction to living beings, and thus You have hundreds and millions of names, like Kṛṣṇa and Govinda. In these tran scendental names You have invested all Your transcendental energies. There are not even hard and fast rules for chanting these names. O my Lord, out of kindness You enable us to easily approach You by Your holy names, but I am so unfortunate that I have no attraction for them."

(*Śikṣāṣṭaka*, 2)

I first met this and seven other verses of *Śikṣāṣṭaka* in 1966, in Śrīla Prabhupāda's Introduction to *Śrīmad-Bhāgavatam*, Canto One, Volume One. At that time I was barely beginning to approach my eternal spiritual master, His Divine Grace A. C. Bhaktivedanta Swami Prabhupāda, and yet I could recognize that the *Śikṣāṣṭaka* verses were very special utterances of devotion to Kṛṣṇa. Śrīla Prabhupāda introduced the *Śikṣāṣṭaka* by stating that the Lord left only eight *ślokas* of His instruction in writing. Moreover, the intense emotions of pure surrender to Kṛṣṇa are so personal and ecstatic that, even if taken as poetry or even when read by a neophyte on the threshold of spiritual life, they are overwhelming. A sentence in the second *śloka* particularly struck me. When Lord Caitanya wrote, "O my Lord, out of kindness You enable us to easily approach You by chanting Your holy names, but I am so unfortunate that I have no attraction for them," I felt He was speaking directly from His heart, and it went directly to my heart. I thought, "How could Lord Caitanya, who has such great love for Kṛṣṇa, speak in this way? How kind He is to mention this unfortunate condition, which is my own!" Over the years I have learned the philosophy of Kṛṣṇa consciousness and taken firmly to its practices, yet this line from *Śikṣāṣṭaka* continues to disarm me and speak to me in the same special way.

If I were to analyze the poetic power of this line, I would say that its great force lies in a dramatic contrast. On the one hand, there is the unlimited kindness and easy accessibility of the holy name. That is expressed by Lord Caitanya with full knowledge and appreciation. *But* the *śloka* ends with His lament, "I am so unfortunate that I have no attachment." Years later, Śrīla Prabhupāda retranslated this *śloka* in the last chapter of *Caitanya-caritāmṛta,* and this time He gave more information as to Lord Caitanya's professed inability to taste the holy name:

> My dear Lord, although You bestow such mercy upon the fallen, conditioned souls by liberally teaching Your holy names, I am so unfortunate that I commit offenses while chanṭing the holy name, and therefore I do not achieve attachment for chanting.

This later version of the verse informs us that the devotee's lack of attachment to the holy name is due to offenses committed while chanting. This revelation only sent the arrow of remorse further into my heart. It was no longer left as a mystery why a chanter does not relish the holy name. It is due to his offenses. We all knew there were ten offenses to the holy name, and thus there was no escaping the unfortunate conclusion given in verse two of *Śikṣāṣṭaka*. In this way, Lord Caitanya's verse laid bare my own failures to appreciate the holy name, and I am sure it has worked effectively in that way for thousands of others. The verse stuns us with its frankness of lament and its confession of personal disqualification, and yet at the same time it offers a special solace.

When in further readings I encountered statements in a similar mood of lamentation, by Lord Caitanya and especially by His followers Kṛṣṇadāsa Kavirāja, Narottama dāsa Ṭhākura and Bhaktivinoda Ṭhākura, I considered them very special and valuable. They were, in one sense, like personal asides from the presentation of the philosophy of the Absolute Truth. And yet because the Kṛṣṇa conscious philosophy is personal and never impersonal, these "statements in which the author describes His fallen condition" were essential and certainly within the philosophical *paramparā*. In presenting my own experiences with verses of this kind, I may not be able to relate them to any direct verbal exchanges I had with Śrīla Prabhupāda (and at present I do not recall many overt adventures in which these verses played part); nevertheless, I know such *ślokas* are my very good friends in Kṛṣṇa consciousness. A person or a verse may be personal in different ways. Some of the verses in this book were personally handed to me or spoken by Śrīla Prabhupāda, and some verses involved me in memorable exchanges with other devotees or nondevotees. Yet some verses we read directly from Śrīla Prabhupāda's books in a quieter but no less crucial way as guides, companions of our inner life, and as strong movers of our spiritual progress. Even while I am very active in the service of my spiritual master, I sometimes have to admit that I don't feel love of Kṛṣṇa. To know at such moments that one is not alone and to receive the assurance and direction of great *ācāryas* is to get renewed courage. It is as if the Vaiṣṇava authors are saying, "Yes, I know how you feel. I feel that way also. Love of God is not so cheap."

I would like to share with my readers several verses by great Vaiṣṇavas which contain similar statements of lamentation. In each instance, we may note that these laments are purifying and thus differ from the materialistic laments of the *śūdra,* who indulges in self-pity. They are also completely different from the hopeless dirges of nondevotees, who can see only suffering and void in a world without Kṛṣṇa. A verse which I encountered in the first printing of *The Nectar of Devotion* is a statement by Rūpa Gosvāmī. Śrīla Prabhupāda quoted it under the heading "Great Hope":

> I have no love for Kṛṣṇa nor for the causes of developing love of Kṛṣṇa—namely, hearing and chanting. And the process of *bhakti-yoga,* by which one is always thinking of Kṛṣṇa and fixing His lotus feet in the heart, is also lacking in me. As far as philosophical knowledge or pious works are concerned, I don't see any opportunity for me to execute such activities. But above all, I am not even born of a nice family. Therefore I must simply pray to You, Gopījanavallabha (Kṛṣṇa, maintainer and beloved of the *gopīs*). I simply wish and hope that some way or other I may be able to approach Your lotus feet, and this hope is giving me pain, because I think myself quite incompetent to approach that transcendental goal of life.

"The purport," Śrīla Prabhupāda writes after presenting this verse, "is that under the heading of *āśā-bandha,* one should continue to hope against hope that some way or other he will be able to approach the lotus feet of the Supreme Lord." I immediately identified with this verse. It was as if Rūpa Gosvāmī were seeing ahead to the time when Western *mlecchas* would become devotees under the guidance of Śrīla Prabhupāda. Rūpa Gosvāmī even spoke of being not born of a nice family, which was actually our lot. "But with so many disqualifications," I thought, "how is it possible to have great hope?" One thing was clear: Rūpa Gosvāmī was not actually a fallen soul. Lord Kṛṣṇa sent him into this world. Śrīla Prabhupāda had even confided to us that Rūpa Gosvāmī was a *gopī mañjarī* in the spiritual world. Rūpa Gosvāmī's purifying lament—like Lord Caitanya's—was for our benefit. And yet Rūpa Go svāmī *did* feel humble and fallen and accused himself of insufficient love for Kṛṣṇa. Therefore, the symptoms of lamentation over lack of love for Kṛṣṇa are simultaneously an expression of the highest stage of devotional service and, when applied to lesser, aspiring devotees, these feelings act as sparks to fan the beginning fire of devotion. They enable us to see what a great, fathomless ocean love of God actually is and how that ocean can be experienced even by the first step into its waves as they extend onto the margin of the land.

Bhaktivinoda Ṭhākura, appearing in the second half of the nineteenth century, has given us a full exposition of feelings of disqualification in spiritual life. In his songs *Śaraṇāgati* ("Surrender"), his expressions go all the way to hopeless despair and beyond. His poems are specifically autobiographical and describe the passage from boyhood through youth to old age. "When I was young," Bhaktivinoda Ṭhākura writes, "I greatly desired to earn money. At that time, bearing in mind the codes of religion, I took a wife." He describes how he increased his family members and spent much time in the "pleasures of mundane learning." He describes an outwardly successful life in which he seems to be enjoying everything that life has to offer, until he realizes, too late, that he has left out the most essential element. "Traveling from place to place," Bhaktivinoda Ṭhākura writes, "I grew wealthy and maintained my family with undivided attention. O Lord Hari, I forgot You!" As he comes to the end of life, he finds he is no longer able to enjoy the senses or to maintain the hope that family and career will be sufficient for happiness. "The current of this worldly river is strong and relentless," Bhaktivinoda Ṭhākura writes. "A frightening, gloomy death approaches. How I wish I could give up my worldly attachments. I would worship You, O Lord, but it is a useless hope."

Describing himself as a conditioned soul, Bhaktivinoda Ṭhākura faces the end of life in depression at the absence of youthful pleasures and increasingly aware that failure in spiritual life is the greatest failure of all. "Were You to judge me now," he writes, "You would find no good qualities. Have mercy and judge me not. Cause me to drink the honey of Your lotus feet and thereby deliver this Bhaktivinoda." After full expressions of hopelessness, the light of great hope at last enters his life with the appearance of a pure devotee, the spiritual master sent as Kṛṣṇa's representative. "A wicked mind brought me into this world, O Lord," Bhaktivinoda Ṭhākura writes, "but one of Your pure and elevated devotees has come to bring me out." Offering him the message of Lord Caitanya, the spiritual master fully revives the broken spirit of Bhaktivinoda Ṭhākura, as he receives the holy name, freely distributed in this age by the *saṅkīrtana* movement of Lord Caitanya. *Śaraṇāgati's* conclusion is victory through the sinner's pure surrender unto the lotus feet of Kṛṣṇa. With great enthusiasm, Bhaktivinoda Ṭhākura offers Lord Kṛṣṇa his active, unconditional surrender. "Mind, body, family, whatever may be mine," he writes, "I have surrendered at Your lotus feet, O youthful son of Nanda!" Totally identifying himself as a servant of the Lord, he no longer considers himself the possessor of anything, yet he offers whatever Kṛṣṇa may have given him to be engaged in the Lord's service. "Nothing remains 'mine,'" writes Bhaktivinoda Ṭhākura, "father, friend, brother—You are even these to me. If I continue to maintain my wealth, family members, home, and wife, it is because they are Yours. I am a mere servant. For Your service I will earn money and bear the expenses of Your household."

As *Śaraṇāgati* plunges to the depths of personal unhappiness, so in conclusion it soars to the heights of personal joy in surrender to Kṛṣṇa. "Unhappiness has gone away," writes Bhaktivinoda Ṭhākura, "and there are no more anxieties. I see joy in all directions." Firmly fixed as the Lord's servant, Bhaktivinoda Ṭhākura states his readiness to be undaunted by any further troubles due to the fear of worldly existence, because now he has found the key to constant happiness. "Troubles encountered in Your service," writes Bhaktivinoda Ṭhākura, "shall be the cause of great happiness, for in Your devotional service joy and sorrow are equally great riches. Both destroy the misery of ignorance."

As the reader enters into Bhaktivinoda Ṭhākura's *Śaraṇāgati,* he realizes that the lamentations of disqualification have been given by Bhaktivinoda Ṭhākura as a blessing upon those of us who are still in the grips of worldliness. But Bhaktivinoda so expertly identifies with the worldly plight that he successfully convinces us to aspire along with him to receive the great hope as distributed by Kṛṣṇa's representative. In this way, the lamentation as expressed in the second *śloka* of *Śikṣāṣṭaka* is fully resolved through pure surrender to Kṛṣṇa as magnanimously described in *Śaraṇāgati.*

The Vaiṣṇava poet Narottama dāsa Ṭhākura, who appeared in the eighteenth century, is another great "king" of purification through lamentation. Although Narottama dāsa has written many Bengali songs on this theme, I will quote only two verses. (I invite the reader, however, to read more fully from Narottama's collection of songs known as *Prārthanā*.)

> Although I sometimes hear the nectarean message of Godhead from the mouths of the devotees, because I commit so many offenses I do not become purified. I continue to associate with nondevotees, and in this way all my spiritual advancement is broken apart. Furthermore, death will soon appear on my horizon.
>
> Although I have repeatedly heard the *śruti* and *smṛti* scriptures' declaration that one should take shelter of the Lord

> Hari's lotus feet in order to become fearless, nevertheless I refuse to happily chant the holy name of Lord Kṛṣṇa, and I decline to meditate on His transcendental form.

In these verses Narottama dāsa Ṭhākura describes how offenses in the practice of devotional life will keep one in a state of lamentation. Especially the seventh offense against the holy name, "to commit sinful activities on the strength of chanting the holy name," will directly work against us. Śrīla Prabhupāda has compared it to the attempt to build a fire and yet throw water upon it. Narottama dāsa sees within himself a stubborn refusal to relent his wrong ways. Thus he has described the plight of the conditioned soul. He knows better; he knows from the *śruti* and *smṛti* that he should surrender and take shelter of Kṛṣṇa, but he refuses. He remains stuck in sinful ways, breaking the principles of religious life. By refusing to meditate on the personal form of the Lord, he commits offenses of impersonalism and agnosticism. "I have spent my life uselessly . . . I have knowingly drunk poison." So what can be done? Although there appears to be no hope, somehow, by the grace of the spiritual master and Kṛṣṇa, Narottama dāsa explains that he will pray and accept the mercy of the Lord. "If you are again merciful," Narottama dāsa Ṭhākura writes, "you will grasp this person by the hair, rescue him from illusion's well, and place him in the abode of Vraja. Seeing that the Lord placed him in an auspicious condition of life, whereas otherwise his life would have perished, the poor and fallen Narottama dāsa sings this song."

The verses of Vaiṣṇava lamentation recognize a soul's fallen nature, but they never endorse it. We cannot quote from these authors and claim, "It is all right if I chant Hare Kṛṣṇa with offenses and never feel any devotional happiness, because Lord Caitanya Mahāprabhu also felt that way." This is bogus reasoning. When Lord Caitanya Mahāprabhu states that He has no attachment for the holy name, that statement is for our benefit only. We should never think that Lord Caitanya or the Vaiṣṇava *ācāryas* are actually offenders. But aside from that, even if we take their statements literally, their lamentations of spiritual anxiety and un happiness are forms of devotional ecstasy. We should not imitate them, however, but rather take their statements as instructions for improving ourselves.

Śrīla Prabhupāda used to tell us on different occasions how Lord Caitanya instructed others by denouncing Himself as a pretender devotee of Kṛṣṇa. One time, when a friend praised Lord Caitanya as the greatest devotee, the Lord said it was not true and that he did not have the slightest devotion to Kṛṣṇa. The friend persisted and said, "Then why is it that I often see You crying tears in devotion?" To this, Lord Caitanya replied that His tears were just imitation so that people would think He was actually a devotee. "If I were actually a devotee," said Lord Caitanya, "then how could I live now that I am in separation from Kṛṣṇa? Kṛṣṇa's not here, and yet I am still living. So how can I claim to have love of Kṛṣṇa?" After hearing such protestations from Lord Caitanya Himself about His lack of devotion, how can any one of us claim that we are actually a great devotee? Thus, the statements by the great Vaiṣṇavas of their lack of devotion also serve the purpose of checking the pride of would-be Vaiṣṇavas who lack true humility.

In a previous essay, "The Boston *Brāhmaṇas*," I quoted verses which argue in favor of the brahminical standing of those born in sinful families and cultures, provided they are properly trained and reformed. Yet these verses of lamentation give us arguments *against* our being sincere devotees. As we need to be encouraged that we may become bona fide devotees despite our birth, so we also need to have our pride checked against thinking we have very easily become great *brāhmaṇas* and ecstatic *bhaktas*. The Vaiṣṇava verses and songs of lamentation give us solace when we see that other devotees are also feeling lowly, yet at the same time they warn us that devotional service is not easily attained and that the failure to attain it is most regrettable. Unless we truly feel grief over our lack of devotion, we can never advance. These songs of lamentation help to open up our hearts so that we may face our own misfortune at not loving Kṛṣṇa. Unless we realize that lack of devotion to Kṛṣṇa is the greatest misfortune in life, we will never see the urgent need for surrendering to Kṛṣṇa. The songs of lamentation, therefore, should not be savored in a dilettantish way. They are meant to turn us to our own selves for an introspective, critical view of our devotional practices. And once we see and admit our failings, then we can attempt to make a rectification, directed by the methods given to us by our spiritual masters.

Throughout the *Śikṣāṣṭaka* the rectification for non-attachment to the holy name of Kṛṣṇa is given in different ways. In the first *śloka* we are advised to take wholeheartedly to the *saṅkīrtana* movement, and we are inspired to hear the all-around spiritual benefits it bestows. In the second *śloka* we are given instructions, according to the transcendental science, that the holy name of Kṛṣṇa is not different from Kṛṣṇa Himself and thus we should chant, confident that the glories of the holy name are real. In the third *śloka* Lord Caitanya gives us a vital instruction about humility. Because we are not attached to the holy name, we should think ourselves lower than the straw in the street and we should offer all respects to others. "In such a state of mind one can chant the holy name of the Lord constantly." This is the major method of reviving our original nature as the servant of the servant of the servant of the Lord.

In the fourth *śloka* Lord Caitanya makes an ideal prayer which we should follow. He prays not for any material benefits, nor even for the benefits of liberation, but for the mercy of "causeless devotional service birth after birth." In this way, Lord Caitanya is introducing us to a pure surrender which asks nothing in return. In the fifth *śloka* Lord Caitanya prays to be picked up from the ocean of death and placed as an atom at the lotus feet of Kṛṣṇa. Although previously He asked for service to the Lord, here He indicates that He does not expect to become equal to the Lord through His service but to be just an infinitesimal particle, serving humbly at the Lord's lotus feet. In the sixth *śloka* Lord Caitanya expresses a desire to attain emotions of love for Kṛṣṇa. When will that day come? (In another verse, in the *Śrīmad-Bhāgavatam,* Śukadeva Gosvāmī states that if emotional symptoms do not take place while we chant, it must mean that our heart is steel-framed. So while we cannot prematurely imitate these emotions, we should understand the meaning of our failure to experience them, and we should aspire to chant humbly and sincerely. Then Kṛṣṇa will be pleased to bestow upon us pure love of God.) In the seventh *śloka* Lord Caitanya expresses feelings of separation from Kṛṣṇa. When the devotee feels Kṛṣṇa's absence, he sees the whole world as a void. If instead we are enamoured by the world of material varieties, while at the same time we do not have an intense service attraction to Kṛṣṇa, then we can never advance in our spiritual life. We have to see the world as void without Kṛṣṇa.

In the eighth and final *śloka* Lord Caitanya expresses the feeling of *ātma-nivedana,* or offering everything one has to Kṛṣṇa. It is the mood of this *śloka* that Bhaktivinoda Ṭhākura has elaborated on in his *Śaraṇāgati* when he declares that he shall give everything to Kṛṣṇa and be happy only to be the Lord's servant, without expectation of reward. Lord Caitanya here expresses pure devotion, without any taint of a business exchange. As long as we are trying to get something from Kṛṣṇa or placing a condition upon our service to Him, then we will not be able to attain His intimate association in the spiritual world. Instead, Kṛṣṇa may give us whatever boon we desire, but not the greatest boon of becoming His intimate servitor. Intimate service to Kṛṣṇa can only be attained when we have no other desire but to serve Him, no matter how He may treat us in exchange.

I find real benefit in hearing the great Vaiṣṇavas' humble statements about their own fallen condition. I know that Kṛṣṇadāsa Kavirāja, Narottama dāsa Ṭhākura, and the other great souls are not actually fallen, and that they are making this expression for our benefit. Yet because I myself am fallen, I can readily identify with this sentiment, and it gives me hope. The Vaiṣṇavas' statements of lamentation are for our purification. By hearing the enumeration of our own sins and lackings which prevent us from advancing in spiritual life, we can have them purged from our hearts once and for all. At least we can increase our desire to do so and increase our determination never to give up trying, never to give up the hope against hope. And in the meantime, we can share in a genuine devotional ecstasy as we join our own hopes to those expressed by Lord Caitanya and the *ācāryas* when they say, "When will that day come when, my offenses ceasing, I will taste the nectar of the holy name?"

XII
Śrīla Prabhupāda's "Favorite" Verse

dharmasya hy āpavargyasya
nārtho 'rthāyopakalpate
nārthasya dharmaikāntasya
kāmo lābhāya hi smṛtaḥ

"All occupational engagements are certainly meant for ultimate liberation. They should never be performed for material gain. Furthermore, according to sages, one who is engaged in the ultimate occupational service should never use material gain to cultivate sense gratification."

(*Bhāg.* 1.2.9)

Did Śrīla Prabhupāda actually have a favorite sastric verse? Was there a verse he considered most important? That's what Professor Thomas Hopkins wanted to find out when he met with Śrīla Prabhupāda in June 1975, at the ISKCON temple in Philadelphia.

Professor Hopkins had always been favorable to the Kṛṣṇa consciousness movement, and so his meeting with Śrīla Prabhupāda was mellow and learned. As a scholar of Hinduism, Professor Hopkins asked Prabhupāda interesting questions, drawing out Śrīla Prabhupāda's realized knowledge of the Vedic conclusions.

"I am collecting material for a sourcebook of readings in Hinduism," said Professor Hopkins, "contemporary as well as classical, and I would like to include in these readings some of the things which you have written. Of that which you have written, what do you consider most important?"

"Premā pum-artho mahān," Śrīla Prabhupāda replied. "The most important thing is how to love God." Professor Hopkins asked where in Prabhupāda's writings did that message of love of God come out most clearly. At first Prabhupāda replied, *"Vedānta* philosophy." But the Professor, looking for a favorite section which he could publish, asked Prabhupāda exactly in what published book that most important message could be found.

"Śrīmad-Bhāgavatam," Prabhupāda replied.

Now that he had narrowed it down to twelve cantos of the *Bhāgavatam,* Professor Hopkins asked, "Which of those books do you consider to be the most important?"

"Well, beginning with the First Canto," said Śrīla Prabhupāda. *"Janmādy asya yataḥ.* Go step by step. First of all, read the *Bhagavad-gītā* nicely, then when we get an idea of the Absolute Truth, then we can study *Śrīmad-Bhāgavatam* more and more."

"But is there any one of the translations or one of the purports or series of purports that you have published that you think is more clear, more . . ."

"Every *śloka* we are describing word to word," said Śrīla Prabhupāda. "So in every *śloka* you will find new ideas. There are eighteen thousand verses."

Professor Hopkins laughed. "I would react the same way," he said, "if anyone asked me a question like that." But keeping his proposed book of readings in mind and wanting a special selection from Śrīla Prabhupāda, Professor Hopkins asked his question again.

"If you were speaking to someone who was going to collect one small section of your work, what would you want them to collect?"

"That is stated in two verses," said Prabhupāda, and he

signaled to his secretary: "Can you find out that book? *Dharmasya hy āpavargyasya nārtho 'rthāyopakalpate.* The first thing is that people should become religious." Śrīla Prabhupāda then launched into an explanation of the *Bhāgavata* philosophy regarding *dharma, artha, kāma,* and *mokṣa.* According to the *Śrīmad-Bhāgavatam,* human civilization begins only when there is *dharma,* or religion, and religion should be pursued not for material benefit but for becoming liberated from the material condition.

When his secretary had found the verse and purport, Prabhupāda asked that he read the purport. The disciple read aloud, and the written purport closely resembled what Śrīla Prabhupāda had just spoken extemporaneously: *"One should not engage himself in any sort of occupational service for material gain only. Nor should material gain be utilized for sense gratification. How material gain should be utilized is described as follows."*

After the purport had been read, Śrīla Prabhupāda continued speaking. "People are after material gain," he said. "They have no spiritual information as to what is the need for spiritual realization. They do not know. Therefore they have been described as *mūḍhas,* fools and rascals, those who are after material gain."

"Do you think then," asked Professor Hopkins, "that that message is the most important message that you have to convey?"

"That is the most important message," said Śrīla Prabhupāda, "because you are not this material body."

Śrīla Prabhupāda was preaching. And specifically, he was speaking to a professor in America. At another time and place, perhaps he would have picked another verse as "the most important message." As he had mentioned earlier, every word of the eighteen thousand verses of *Śrīmad-Bhāgavatam* is absolute and perfect. But as a preacher, according to person, time, and place, he had picked out an important verse.

The *Bhāgavatam* verse beginning *dharmasya hy āpavargasya* was most important because it stressed a very basic point—the real identity of the self, and the real purpose of religion. Unless one understood these basic things, how could he go on to anything else "more important"? Since throughout the whole material world (and Prabhupāda had personally seen most of it) almost everyone was engaged in taking care of the body, and no one knew the nature of spirit soul, the most important thing was to provide education about the self.

"Therefore in your country," said Śrīla Prabhupāda, "in every country, it is blind education, no spiritual enlightenment."

"What is the solution?" asked Professor Hopkins. "Devotion to God?"

"First of all you know what is spirit," replied Śrīla Prabhupāda, "then as soon as you know that you are spirit, then wherefrom the spirit comes? Or wherefrom everything comes? When you ask that, then you can come to the question of God. And then we understand what is our relationship with God. And if we act according to that, then we will find perfect life."

"So you would then see the *Bhagavad-gītā* as a guide to understand?" said Professor Hopkins.

Prabhupāda agreed and said that the very first lessons of the *Bhagavad-gītā,* beginning in Chapter Two, were given to Arjuna because he was lamenting in the bodily concept of life.

Although Professor Hopkins managed to secure a "most important" verse from Śrīla Prabhupāda, he could see that the discussion could not be contained to the selection of an author's favorite. Śrīla Prabhupāda was not a connoisseur of the Vedic literatures in a merely literary or academic sense. The *śāstras* were to Śrīla Prabhupāda a living, flowing continuum. As a preacher, he selected as his favorites the most important verses for discussion according to the necessity of time, place, and person. From experience and realization Śrīla Prabhupāda was expert in this, and he applied it continually, both in his written works and in his almost constant speaking of Kṛṣṇa consciousness as he traveled from country to country. It is very difficult to take a single verse and frame it and hang it on the wall as "the most important Vedic verse according to Śrīla Prabhupāda." Prabhupāda's "most important" was always preaching itself, glorifying Kṛṣṇa in pure devotion, and extending His mercy to whomever he met.

Śrīla Prabhupāda used individual verses in different ways. In his presentation of *Easy Journey to Other Planets,* he even changed some of the translated words of the *Bhagavad-gītā* verses and inserted scientific jargon, such as "anti-material," to get his message across to the scientists. He did not deviate in any way from the message of the *Bhagavad-gītā,* but he *taught it* to his selected audience.

Śrīla Prabhupāda knew by memory hundreds of verses, and in his writing he referred to all of the available *śāstras* and commentaries of the *ācāryas*. Out of this vast body of knowledge, he constantly called upon different verses as he needed them. His favorites were not a static group, but he varied them according to his audience. For example, a favorite verse when speaking to an Indian audience might be *bhārata-bhūmite haila manuṣya-janma yāra,* which stresses that anyone born in the land of India has a special duty to distribute the instructions of Vedic knowledge. A most important verse when speaking to a congregation in a Western church might concern the concept of *sanātana-dharma*. And a most important verse for inclusion in a professor's reading anthology might be *dharmasya hy āpavargyasya*.

On another occasion, Śrīla Prabhupāda's leading book

distributor disciple, Tripurāri Mahārāja, asked Prabhupāda which was the most important book to distribute to the nondevotees. At first Śrīla Prabhupāda said, "The *Bhagavad-gītā*." When a devotee asked, "What about *Īśopaniṣad*?" Prabhupāda replied, "Yes, that also." Another devotee asked, "And the *Kṛṣṇa* book?" Prabhupāda also approved that. Then he himself added, "*Śrīmad-Bhāgavatam* and *The Nectar of Devotion*." The book distributors began to laugh, seeing that Prabhupāda really considered all of his books as favorites and as worthy of being studied by the nondevotee public.

Devotees once asked Prabhupāda if he would tell them which of the Rādhā-Kṛṣṇa Deities in his ISKCON temples were his favorite. Prabhupāda replied, "If I selected one, that would be my sense gratification." He seemed to not want to make a distinction of one Kṛṣṇa over another, since They were all absolute. Similarly, we might conjecture that Śrīla Prabhupāda would be hesitant to say which of the verses composed by Śrīla Vyāsadeva was the most important, since every word of the *Bhāgavatam* is considered "the breathing of Nārāyāṇā."

Transcribers of Śrīla Prabhupāda's lectures have made mathematical notations of the frequency in which Prabhupāda used different verses in his lectures. Among the verses he most often turned to was *sarva-dharmān parityajya mām ekaṁ śaraṇaṁ vraja:* "Abandon all varieties of religion and surrender unto Me. I will release you from the reactions to sin. Do not be afraid." But can we say that was his favorite? And if we asked him now, what would he say? Would we get a reply similar to Professor Hopkins', according to time, person, and place? Rather than conjecture, we had better remember another sastric reference, which states, "One should never attempt to know the mind of the Vaiṣṇava." I can recall Prabhupāda's immediate reply when Professor Hopkins asked him for the most important verse.

"*Prema pum-artho mahān,*" said Prabhupāda. "Love of Kṛṣṇa is the most important thing."

XIII

Verses as Weapons

ye 'nye 'ravindākṣa vimukta-māninas
tvayy asta-bhāvād aviśuddha-buddhayaḥ
āruhya kṛcchreṇa paraṁ padaṁ tataḥ
patanty adho 'nādṛta-yuṣmad-anghrayaḥ

"[Someone may say that aside from devotees, who always seek shelter at the Lord's lotus feet, there are those who are not devotees but who have accepted different processes for attaining salvation. What happens to them? In answer to this question, Lord Brahmā and the other demigods said:] O lotus-eyed Lord, although nondevotees who accept severe austerities and penances to achieve the highest position may think themselves liberated, their intelligence is impure. They fall down from their position of imagined superiority because they have no regard for Your lotus feet."

(*Bhāg.* 10.2.32)

I first became acquainted with this verse by hearing phrases from it, or sometimes the first or second half of the verse, in Śrīla Prabhupāda's lectures. Phrases like *vimukta-māninaḥ* and *āruhya kṛcchreṇa* stayed in my mind as unidentified, absolute sound vibration, and I was finally able to put it all together when I saw the complete verse in one of Śrīla Prabhupāda's printed purports. Some of his scholarly disciples had also memorized it and used it in their lectures, and

I began also. In a four-line barrage this verse stops the claim that a meditator can gain eternal liberation by meditation on the impersonal Brahman. Because the philosophy of impersonalism, as enunciated by Śaṅkarācārya, is very influential around the world, it is important for Vaiṣṇava preachers to be aware of the basic sastric references like this one, which clarifies the issue of personalism and impersonalism.

I personally heard and saw Śrīla Prabhupāda use this entire verse, or its parts, in many public lectures. With the phrase *vimukta-māninaḥ* he pointed out that the impersonalists' claim to be liberated from material identity is only a mental concoction, a "liberation in mind only." With the phrase *aviśuddha-buddhayaḥ* he made it bluntly clear that liberation without Kṛṣṇa consciousness is a claim by one whose intelligence is still not purified. With the phrase *āruhya kṛcchreṇa* he acknowledged that impersonal meditators may achieve a very high state of consciousness after performing severe austerities, and they may even merge into the Brahman effulgence in the spiritual sky after leaving their bodies at death. But unfortunately for the impersonalists, the phrase *patanty adhaḥ* describes their inevitable falldown again into material existence. And why does this falldown await them, even after their long austerities and their merging into Brahman? Because, *anādṛta-yuṣmad-aṅghrayaḥ:* they have neglected to worship the lotus feet of Lord Kṛṣṇa, the Supreme Personality of Godhead.

On a morning walk in Boston in 1968, I heard Śrīla Prabhupāda quote this verse in a way that I will never forget. For several mornings, some students of a popular *haṭha-yoga* swami accompanied Śrīla Prabhupāda on his morning walk. They asked questions in an attempt to understand the difference between their impersonal *yoga* practices and the path of *bhakti-yoga*. When Śrīla Prabhupāda mentioned that only by surrender to Kṛṣṇa could one attain eternal liberation in the spiritual sky, one of the *haṭha-yoga* students wanted to know the exact origin of this assertion.

"Does it actually say anywhere *in the scriptures,*" the *yoga* student asked, "that you have to come back to the material world if you don't worship Kṛṣṇa? Does it actually say it?"

"Yes, yes," said Prabhupāda, and he quoted, *"āruhya kṛcchreṇa paraṁ padaṁ tataḥ patanty adho 'nadṛtayuṣmad-aṅghrayaḥ:* 'By neglecting Your lotus feet, he has to come down again.'" Then in a loud, emphatic voice, Prabhupāda added, "Feet! *Feet means He is a person!*" Not only were the *yoga* students startled by Prabhupāda's assertion, but I also jumped to a new awareness about the lotus feet of Kṛṣṇa and the regretful neglect caused by impersonal speculation.

Ye 'nye 'ravindākṣa is a strong stopper, and there are many other sastric references which stop the advance of doctrines contrary to the Vaiṣṇava conclusion. The devotee preacher learns to use these Vedic verses and arguments as weapons in his going forth to preach on behalf of Kṛṣṇa consciousness. As he regularly meets opposition, either from the camp of those who take shelter in the *Vedas,* such as the Māyāvādīs, or from those atheists who reject the scriptures and take shelter in logical argument, the well-trained Vaiṣṇava is never silenced or defeated. In a *Bhāgavatam* purport concerning the debate between the Viṣṇudūtas and the Yamadūtas, Prabhupāda stresses the need for devotees to thoroughly know the philosophy of Kṛṣṇa consciousness — "otherwise they will be considered foolish." Śrīla Prabhupāda writes: "All the devotees, especially preachers, must know the philosophy of Kṛṣṇa consciousness so as not to be embarrassed and insulted when they preach." (*Bhāg*. 6.1.38, purport)

The need for fighting is also mentioned in the *Kṛṣṇa* book chapter "The Teachings of the Personified *Vedas,*" which contains many intricate arguments against impersonalism. There, Śrīla Prabhupāda explains that by their own inclinations, devotees like to peacefully and agreeably chant and hear about the glories of Kṛṣṇa in the company of pure devotees. But if someone comes to challenge Kṛṣṇa consciousness—which often happens in this world of devotees and demons—the Vaiṣṇava must be prepared to defeat the opposition with sastric knowledge.

Bhaktisiddhānta Sarasvatī Ṭhākura was renowned for his "axe preaching," and Māyāvādī teachers used to try to avoid him, for fear of getting a beating. Bhaktisiddhānta Sarasvatī did not like his disciples to compromise the philosophy, and therefore he gave his fullest blessings to his boldest preacher, His Divine Grace A.C. Bhaktivedanta Swami Prabhupāda, who had the courage to travel to the countries of the demons for establishing Kṛṣṇa consciousness worldwide. Like his spiritual master, Śrīla Prabhupāda was a formidable fighter, and he sometimes described his mission in military terms. He said that his disciples should be good soldiers, and they should go out and distribute books, just as in wartime the planes rain down bombs like anything. He said that when he published a new book he felt as if he had conquered an empire. And when his movement was brought to court on charges of "brainwashing," Prabhupāda responded by ordering his disciples to bring all of his books into court and demand that the judge and lawyers read them before passing judgment.

In India, where the Vedic scriptures are still widely respected (as well as abused), many key verses were used as stoppers by Śrīla Prabhupāda. In fact, the entire *Bhagavad-gītā* is a stopper against all anti-Kṛṣṇa conclusions; it cannot logically be used to support any position short of complete surrender to Kṛṣṇa. Any devotee, therefore, who is well acquainted with the *Bhagavad-gītā* can withstand the onslaught of the atheists and Māyāvādīs and go on to convince people of the necessity of surrender to Kṛṣṇa as the Supreme Personality of Godhead. I once heard a *sannyāsī* disciple ask Śrīla Prabhupāda for advice for preaching in the south of India, which is well known for its *paṇḍitas* learned in the scriptures. Śrīla Prabhupāda said that if the *sannyāsī* disciple could learn only thirty key verses in the *Bhagavad-gītā,* that would be enough for meeting any challenges from the South Indian *paṇḍitas*. Such is the conclusive strength of the *Bhagavad-gītā*.

I would like to here state just a few *Bhagavad-gītā* preaching references on important themes, as I have heard them used by Śrīla Prabhupāda. One important theme for a preacher to establish conclusively is that Kṛṣṇa is the Supreme Godhead. For this, Prabhupāda would quote almost without fail *mattaḥ parataraṁ nānyat* (Bg. 7.7): "There is no truth superior to Me." Another undeniable evidence of Kṛṣṇa's supremacy is *ahaṁ sarvasya prabhavaḥ* (Bg. 10.8): "I am the source of all material and spiritual worlds; everything emanates from Me." And if one questions whether Kṛṣṇa is just another demigod, there is, among others, the *Gītā* phrase *aham ādir hi devānām* (Bg. 10.2): "I am the source of the demigods and sages."

It is also not difficult to establish that *bhakti-yoga* is the supreme path, based on key *Bhagavad-gītā* verses. If one considers *yoga,* then he should know the conclusion of *yoga* and its ultimate success. Lord Kṛṣṇa declares, *yoginam api sarveṣām*: "And of all *yogīs,* the one with great faith who always abides in Me, thinks of Me within himself, and renders transcendental loving service to Me—he is the most intimately united with Me in *yoga,* and he is the highest of all." (Bg. 6.47) Or if one wants to consider the path of *karma,* the conclusion is the same: *yat karoṣi yad aśnāsi:* "Whatever you do, whatever you eat, whatever you offer or give away, and whatever austerities you perform, do that, O son of Kuntī, as an offering to Me." (Bg. 9.27) Action in Kṛṣṇa consciousness is the supreme activity. If one considers that knowledge, or *jñāna,* is the supreme path, then he should know what is the supreme *jñāna*. Lord Kṛṣṇa declares, *bahūnāṁ janmanām ante:* "After many births and deaths, he who is actually in knowledge surrenders unto Me, knowing Me to be the cause of all causes and all that is. Such a great soul is very rare." (Bg. 7.19)

Although Māyāvādī philosophers attempt to use the *Bhagavad-gītā* in nefarious ways, the conclusion in favor of personalism is unavoidable. This is particularly striking and decisive in the opening verses of the twelfth chapter. Here Arjuna specifically and directly asks Kṛṣṇa what is considered to be more perfect, "those who are always properly engaged in the devotional service of Lord Kṛṣṇa or those who worship the impersonal Brahman or unmanifested." Lord Kṛṣṇa's reply is equally clear and direct: "The Supreme Personality of Godhead said: Those who fix their minds on My personal form and are always engaged in worshiping Me with great and transcendental faith are considered by Me to be most perfect." (Bg. 12.2) In the next verse Kṛṣṇa says that those who "fully worship the unmanifested . . . the impersonal conception of the Absolute Truth . . . at last achieve Me." (Bg. 12.3–4)

Of course, most atheists do not accept any scripture, Vedic or otherwise. The preacher must therefore meet their challenges in a different way. Although the Absolute Truth can never be ascertained simply by mundane arguments, a devotee may have to engage in logic in order to establish the Absolute Truth. This method is approved by the example of Lord Caitanya Mahāprabhu, who defeated the Buddhists in argument. Śrīla Prabhupāda comments on this pastime of Lord Caitanya and its application for devotees of the modern day:

> Those who are preachers in ISKCON will certainly meet many people who believe in intellectual arguments. Most of these people do not believe in the authority of the Vedas.

> Nevertheless, they accept intellectual speculation and argument. Therefore the preacher of Kṛṣṇa consciousness should be prepared to defeat others by argument, just as Śrī Caitanya Mahāprabhu did. In this verse it is clearly said, *tarkei khaṇḍila prabhu*. Lord Śrī Caitanya Mahāprabhu put forward such a strong argument that they could not counter Him to establish their cult.
>
> (Cc. *Mādhya* 9.49)

As Lord Caitanya defeated various atheists of His day by logical argument, so Śrīla Prabhupāda was the first Vaiṣṇava *ācārya* to stop the modern scientists. He engaged in many scientific arguments, often with his disciple Dr. Svarūpa Dāmodara, who was himself a scientist.

On hearing the scientists' claim that life comes from matter, Prabhupāda replied, "I say to the scientists, 'If life originated from chemicals, and if your science is so advanced, then why can't *you* create life biochemically in the laboratories?' "

On hearing the scientists' claims that they would create life "in the future," Prabhupāda said this was like trying to pass a post-dated check.

When he heard that many scientists were in disagreement about the definition of *living* and *nonliving*, Prabhupāda replied, "Because somebody is saying one thing and somebody else is saying another, their knowledge must be imperfect."

When Prabhupāda heard that according to Nobel Laureate Dr. J. Monod chemicals were created by chance, and then necessity arose and molecules reoriented themselves, Prabhupāda replied, "If everything was happening by chance, how can there be necessity?"

When he heard the scientists' claim that there is no life on the moon, Prabhupāda replied, "They are thinking limitedly, in terms of their own circumstances. This is called 'Dr. Frog's philosophy.' " (Dr. Frog is a foolish, figurative frog, who on hearing of the existence of the Pacific Ocean attempted to judge the length and depth of the ocean based on his empirical knowledge of his own ten-foot well.) Śrīla Prabhupāda was not only defensive in stopping the scientists' atheistic theories, but he was also aggressive. "They have discovered atomic energy," he said. "Now they can kill millions at once. They have simply cleared the way for death. And yet they dare to declare that they will make life!"

In similar ways, Śrīla Prabhupāda employed simple but brilliant logical stoppers to various non-Vaiṣṇava theories. He sometimes played the part of antagonist and invited his disciples to defeat him. One morning he spoke as a pious religionist and said he had no need to hear about Kṛṣṇa consciousness, since he was already a lover of God. When Prabhupāda's disciples argued with him that he did not know the full science of God, Prabhupāda replied that whatever he knew was sufficient and that he loved God in his own way. After his disciples' unsuccessful attempt to defeat their spiritual master with different arguments, Prabhupāda finally supplied the logical argument that they were looking for. "If you actually love God," said Śrīla Prabhupāda, "then you must obey Him. Without obedience there is no love." He then went on to describe the basic commandments of God consciousness, including "Thou shalt not kill," and then he proceeded to expose the sinfulness of those who slaughter and eat animals.

Prabhupāda was almost always engaged in some kind of dialectical discourse, and in this way he eminently followed in the footsteps of the previous *ācāryas* like Madhvācārya, Rāmanujācārya, and his own spiritual master, Bhaktisiddhānta Sarasvatī Ṭhākura. And Prabhupāda expected the same from his own followers, those who would attempt to establish and spread Kṛṣṇa consciousness under his instruction.

Our conclusion is that preachers are fighters. They feel enlivened when they meet opposition and when they successfully defend Kṛṣṇa consciousness. Feeling the power of the Vaiṣṇava philosophy as well as the emotions of loyalty which arise when faithfully uttering Lord Kṛṣṇa's teachings, a devotee experiences great joy. When attacks and abuses appear to set back the Kṛṣṇa consciousness movement, a sincere devotee will see these as opportunities to fight back by speaking against *māyā*. Nor is his fighting a mere exercise for pleasure, but it is a mission for delivering the unfortunate souls of this age who are caught up in the network of illusion and are suffering at the hands of demoniac manipulators. And to conduct this fighting on behalf of Kṛṣṇa, a devotee has to use his many verses as weapons. In the course of fighting for Kṛṣṇa, a devotee also banishes the demoniac enemies within his own mind, as a happy by-product. When the *ślokas* fly from the bow of a competent preacher, along with quick-flying, inspiring arguments of logic, the forces of *māyā* fall back in bewilderment. Lord Kṛṣṇa assures the preachers, just as he assures his warrior-devotee Arjuna, "The doubts which have arisen in your heart out of ignorance should be slashed by the weapon of knowledge. Armed with *yoga,* O Bhārata, stand and fight."

XIV
Things Undertaken Without Kṛṣṇa Fail

asuryā nāma te lokā
andhena tamasāvṛtāḥ
tāṁs te pretyābhigacchanti
ye ke cātma-hano janāḥ

"The killer of the soul, whoever he may be, must enter into the planets known as the worlds of the faithless, full of darkness and ignorance.

PURPORT

"The modern soul-killing civilization has only increased the problems of a hungry stomach. We approach some polished animal, a modern civilized man, and he says that he wants to work for the satisfaction of the stomach and there is no necessity for self-realization. But the laws of Nature are so cruel that in spite of his eagerness to work hard for his stomach, there is always the question of unemployment, even after denouncing the prospect of self-realization.

"We are given this human form of life not to work hard like the ass, the swine, and the dog, but to attain the highest perfection of life. If we do not care for self-realization, it is by the law of nature that we have to work very hard even though we do not want to do so. . . . The conclusion is that we are not meant only for solving economic problems on a tottering platform, but we are also meant for solving the problems of the material life into which we have been placed by the conditions of Nature."

(*Śrī Īśopaniṣad, Mantra* 3)

The theme of this essay involves my ongoing struggle to understand and carry out a particular instruction from Śrīla Prabhupāda, and I have somewhat arbitrarily selected a verse from the *Īśopaniṣad* to illustrate this theme. This is not an untypical way in which Vedic verses come to our minds or enter into our lives. In fact, it is one of the most absorbing and productive ways to study Prabhupāda's books. Yet before I complete this short story about an unfulfilled task, I will also clarify why I have selected the *mantra* about the killers of the soul.

"You are writing a book?" Śrīla Prabhupāda asked me. I sat before him in his room within the Detroit mansion. This was in June 1976. If I had been startled when Prabhupāda's servant awoke me at 10:00 P.M., I was even more surprised to come before Śrīla Prabhupāda and hear him ask me if I was writing a book. My first response was shame and fear. I thought Śrīla Prabhupāda was now going to reprimand me for my audacity in daring to write a book. Śrīla Prabhupāda's gaze was loving but exposed all sham.

"Yes," I confessed, "I wrote that book, *Readings in Vedic Literature*."

"That book is completed," said Śrīla Prabhupāda with a gesture, and then I realized he was not going to reprimand me. "I want you to write another book," he said. "It should be about why things undertaken without Kṛṣṇa fail." I nodded with eager expectation and clutched for the little notebook in my *kurtā* pocket. Śrīla Prabhupāda explained that in India the government had recently planned to build an ideal city, but now the whole scheme had collapsed as a farce. It had failed for lack of Kṛṣṇa consciousness. There were similar examples. I could write a book about it.

"Like the U.N.?" I asked, hoping to catch his idea. Prabhupāda had often given the example that the U.N.'s purpose was to preserve peace and unity among nations, but since their formation there had been continuous wars, and instead of creating world unity, "simply the flags outside the U.N. are always increasing."

Śrīla Prabhupāda replied, "Yes, that is another example."

"And Gandhi?" I asked. Prabhupāda responded to that by speaking further about Gandhi. He said that at the end of his life Gandhi felt all of his plans for nonviolence, national unity, and the promotion of village culture had been thwarted. The talk then enlarged to criticism of the world leaders, who are actually *asuras,* and who harass people unnecessarily in the name of government. He said that real government should be *īśavāsya,* God-centered, but in the Kali-yuga the leaders would become so oppressive that eventually people would abandon civilized living due to droughts and too much tax, and they would go and live in the hills. It was the devotees' duty, said Śrīla Prabhupāda, to point out the real purpose of life, but when we do so they say they are not interested. They take it as religion, whereas they are interested in economic development. And yet whatever they attempt they fail, because they are without Kṛṣṇa.

After an hour of related discussion, Śrīla Prabhupāda told me to go take rest. I thanked him and went to lie down on the floor of our mobile home parked outside the temple. But it was hard to sleep now. I was thrilled at being called by Śrīla Prabhupāda for a late, private *darśana* and being asked to write a book. The writing project reminded me of a similar assignment I had heard Śrīla Prabhupāda give to his disciple Bhagavān Goswami when Prabhupāda was in Italy and then France in 1974. During several morning walks Śrīla

Prabhupāda had described how various problems of the world could be solved by the application of Kṛṣṇa consciousness. He said that Bhagavān should write a book about it. Devotees like Yogeśvara and Hari-vilāsa had entered into the spirit of Prabhupāda's talk and introduced different world problems for Prabhupāda to comment upon. On the topic of international terrorism, Prabhupāda said that people should not expect to do away with terrorism as long as the vast majority of human beings were behaving as animals. If one ferocious beast fights with another in the jungle, he said, we should not be surprised. Similarly, as long as humanity lived as animals, without knowledge of selfrealization, then we could not expect an end to terroristic violence. On the subject of divorce, Śrīla Prabhupāda humorously remarked, "Don't get married. Remain *brahmacārī*. That is the solution." Making impromptu but sastric-based comments about many world problems, Śrīla Prabhupāda asked his disciples to elaborate on them in a book and in articles for *Back to Godhead* magazine. Even at that time I had wished that Prabhupāda had given me the assignment of writing the book, and now, years later, he had turned to me also.

Busy months passed by and I never began the book. I could not find time to do it, and whenever I thought of the project, large obstacles seemed to present themselves. I was afraid the book would appear dogmatic and simplistic if we just took one world dilemma after another and said that the solution was "Chant Hare Kṛṣṇa and surrender to Kṛṣṇa." Yet that was our conviction—relief would come only if all sections of humanity surrendered to Kṛṣṇa and took up the chanting of His holy names. But it seemed that readers, especially in the West, would demand more explanation. Specialized experts all agreed that the world's current crises and problems were intricate and complex, with no easy solutions. Readers would see our summary analysis as naive.

Perhaps it meant that I would have to first become an expert in each field. How could I discuss with historical accuracy exactly what went wrong with the U.N. unless I knew as much about the U.N. as the experts? But how detailed would my studies have to be? And where was the time to do such things along with my many other heavy duties in ISKCON? Maybe Prabhupāda intended that we only present the principles of Kṛṣṇa consciousness. But if in chapter after chapter we dealt with subjects like nuclear arms control, world economy, and education, and repeatedly said only that the answer to the problem is to become Kṛṣṇa conscious, then what hard-core materialist would accept it? Of course, I had the example of Śrīla Prabhupāda's own preaching as founder-*ācārya* of the Kṛṣṇa consciousness movement. But I did not think I could imitate him. I did not yet have a grasp of what to do in order to write *Things Undertaken Without Kṛṣṇa Fail*. I asked different Godbrothers who had various ideas of how such a book could be written. When I brought up to them what I considered the problems of such a presentation, they admitted it sounded difficult but that it could be done by Prabhupāda's grace.

In early 1977, Śrīla Prabhupāda assigned me to return as editor-in-chief of his *Back to Godhead* magazine. I went to Los Angeles, and while working on the monthly magazine, I was able to think more about the book. In time, I decided that the book should contain chapters describing different world schemes and how each of them failed. I recalled that Prabhupāda and I had discussed the U.N. and Gandhi, and so I decided that I should first acquaint myself with the life and works of Gandhi. In the library I immediately found many biographies and analyses of his life's work. Days went by, and after many hours of reading I felt overwhelmed. Just to understand Gandhi and his times could become the work of a lifetime! And yet I was supposed to become equally knowledgeable in a whole range of fields! In June, I wrote to Śrīla Prabhupāda asking him what to do. I had produced scores of pages of struggling notes yet had no clear direction or feeling of confidence.

By this time Prabhupāda had retired from traveling and from active participation in the management of his movement. "Now I am in my last days," he said. Sensing the end of his mortal life, Prabhupāda had gradually stopped eating, and in May 1977, all of the G.B.C. members were called to Vṛndāvana, where they expected the worst. At the urgent pleading of his leading disciples, Prabhupāda began to again make efforts to eat and to sustain himself, and it appeared that his health had somewhat recovered. By the time my letter arrived, Prabhupāda was again speaking daily to his secretary, Tamāl Kṛṣṇa Goswami, who would send us Prabhupāda's responses to our letters. Early in July, I received Tamāl Kṛṣṇa's reply:

> My dear Satsvarupa Maharaja,
>
> Please accept my most humble obeisances at your feet. I have been instructed by His Divine Grace Srila Prabhupada to reply to your letter dated June 28, 1977. Yes, Srila Prabhupada was very pleased with the Ratha-yatra issue of Back to Godhead. Srila Prabhupada was pleased that you were thinking of the magazine as a tool for making new devotees. He said, "Making new devotees means success of preaching."
>
> Regarding the proposed book on the theme, "things undertaken without Krsna fail," His Divine Grace commented at length about this. Srila Prabhupada said, "I think that it is not a good idea. You should go positively forward instead of attacking others. It will create a section of enemies. If we attack so many people, then we will have to fight with everyone one after another. What is the use? They are failures. That is a fact. Failure is failure. Let us prove by action that all others are failures. Just alike all yogis is a failure now. Transcendental Meditation is going to be a failure. To criticize means to give some important rival Hare Krsna. Don't write such book. It will be embarrassment. When I am asked, 'Do you know such and such person?' I say, 'I do not know such person.' This way I

give no importance at all. Our criticism is that as soon as we see there is no Krsna consciousness, it is rejected. A rascal is beautiful so long as he doesn't speak. As soon as he speaks you can understand. Just like rice. Press a piece, and if it is not soft, you can understand that it is all uncooked. Similarly, one word like 'probably' [this refers to an atlas in which so many of the statements were preceded by the word 'probably'], that means they are finished. There is a proverb in Bengali: 'If you kill a skunk, your hand gets a bad smell. If you attack others, some bad smell will be there. I never did so. Keep your position respectable. Don't create many enemies. Why should I try to understand Gandhi and Ramakrishna philosophy? I know from beginning it is useless, no importance. I therefore say, 'I do not know these.' Let others present the philosophy of Ramakrishna or Gandhi, and then you smash it. You crush it by kicking. Otherwise your hand will get a bad smell. [In other words, when others bring up the name Gandhi, you can ask, 'What is his philosophy?' After it is described, then you can smash it.] I am concentrating on three books: Bhagavad-gita As It Is, Srimad-Bhagavatam, and Caitanya-caritamrta. All other small books are based on these three in one way or another. In the condition of life that I am in I try to write books. If I cannot sleep all right, then let me write. Even if two lines. What is the use of wasting time?"

Regarding Ratha-yatra, Srila Prabhupada had this to say: "If we introduce Ratha-yatra in every city, all other religions will be finished."

Srila Prabhupada was very appreciative of the review of Readings in Vedic Literature. Regarding the BBT's first prize for the most attractive booth at the American Library Association, Srila Prabhupada declared, "This is a triumph."

Jaya, Maharaja. Hoping this meets you well.

Your servant,
Tamal Krishna Goswami
servant of Srila Prabhupada

Śrīla Prabhupāda had really smashed me. And he saved me from a disastrous mistake: I had been attempting to kill a skunk with my hand. I needed no further warning to avoid studying the lives of great misleaders or to avoid writing about them by name. But Prabhupāda's criticism was so heavy and lengthy! It made me think that the whole "proposed book" was "not a good idea." Is that what he meant? His comments at the end seemed to indicate that books about material subjects were just a waste of time. Better we write straight sastric-based works, like Prabhupāda's own translation of *Śrīmad-Bhāgavatam*. That was how he had always directed me to write for *Back to Godhead*—simple, straightforward explanations of Kṛṣṇa consciousness. Yes, we should expose the demons as fools and rascals and introduce instead the real philosophy as Lord Kṛṣṇa teaches. But this should not be done by becoming too much entangled in explaining materialistic philosophy. I recalled how in the old days of BTG, Rayarāma dāsa would write book reviews of Herman Hesse and Martin Buber. Prabhupāda stopped it, saying that we should not give them free advertisements. Yet he had praised *Readings in Vedic Literature*, in which I had quoted academic scholars. It is a thin line between right and wrong, and I had certainly been mistaken to plow into the works of Gandhi and other leaders and world projects. I had to think more about the book.

In my mind, the project became mixed with my anxiety over the threat of Prabhupāda's disappearance. There was no direct connection between the two, but by writing I had tried to absorb myself and "do something," so as not to get lost myself in thinking about what would happen if Prabhupāda left, or whether I should again go to India to be with him.

But I did not want to just drop the whole project, and so I tried again. I scanned through all of Śrīla Prabhupāda's books and took out references to the *varṇāśrama-dharma* system, the division of humanity into four social and four spiritual orders. I felt that a dissertation on the Vedic social system would be an overall way to answer the questions as to why there were so many problems in human society. The problems are due to not having a sane, spiritual organization. When Rāmeśvara Swami, the BBT trustee in Los Angeles, heard that I was working on a book on *varṇāśrama-dharma,* he became excited and encouraged me about its importance for preaching. In August, when I was again able to visit Śrīla Prabhupāda in Vṛndāvana, I carried with me the quotes about *varṇāśrama.*

Even during Śrīla Prabhupāda's last weeks and days I continued to write about *varṇāśrama-dharma* in a room in the Krishna-Balaram guesthouse. Sometimes I would go and chant soft *kīrtana* before Śrīla Prabhupāda in his darkened room, but after a few hours I would become restless and return to my room to make notes in my diary or look at my *varṇāśrama-dharma* quotes. But by now, everything had begun to confuse and disinterest me. Why was I struggling with this literary project, which seemed to go nowhere, while Prabhupāda was disappearing? Why wasn't I spending more time personally serving Śrīla Prabhupāda while he was still with us? Why wasn't I down in his room at least chanting with him? The "proposed book" became merged into the mental strain and dullness of consciousness which some of us experienced in Prabhupāda's last days.

After the unforgettable time of Śrīla Prabhupāda's disappearance, we devotees returned to our fields of work, absorbed in sadness at the loss of our best friend, but determined to serve him in separation. I began work on the lectures later published as *He Lives Forever* and carried out my duties of traveling, preaching, and producing *Back to Godhead.* During the ensuing months, ISKCON became caught up in discussions about Śrīla Prabhupāda's appointment of initiating *gurus* and how they would actually carry out their duties. I also began thinking about a biography of Śrīla Prabhupāda. My *varṇāśrama-dharma* book was not only taken off the back burner but removed from the stove.

Now, years later, our highly-qualified Godbrother Harīkeśa Swami Viṣṇupāda has published his revolutionary and comprehensive volume *Varṇāśrama Manifesto for Social Sanity*. In his book he has fully described the need for a *varṇāśrama* society and the functions of the four orders, the *brāhmaṇas,* the *kṣatriyas,* the *vaiśyas,* and the *śūdras*. He has also analyzed the false foundations of modern society, as well as many particular anomalies, such as the mistakes of modern science, and he has predicted how in the future a Vaiṣṇava *varṇāśrama* world-order can come about. So he has already done the job.

But my story does not end there. I cannot simply say, "Somebody else did it, so I am off the hook." Rather, in time I have come to understand that it is not just the writing of one book that Śrīla Prabhupāda requested that night in Detroit. He was requesting many books and many articles in *Back to Godhead*. And he was requesting more than book writing, also. Prabhupāda was talking about the entire mission of Kṛṣṇa consciousness and how to implement it in today's world. People think that Kṛṣṇa consciousness is not at all important or that it is merely "religious." Devotees in the Kṛṣṇa consciousness movement have to convince them that we can actually solve their problems. During my travels with Śrīla Prabhupāda, I had seen him expertly do this.

At a press conference in Hyderabad, a reporter asked Prabhupāda a technical, theological question—whether he was an *advaita* (monistic) or a *dvaita* (dualistic) philosopher. Śrīla Prabhupāda scoffed at the question. "What is the point of discussing such things," Prabhupāda said, "whether one is *dvaita* or *advaita*? Kṛṣṇa says, *annād bhavanti bhūtāni*: 'All living beings subsist on food grains.' So the people have no grains. But the grains are produced from rain, and the rain is from *yajña*. So perform *yajña,* become Kṛṣṇa conscious. Whether you are *dvaita* or *advaita,* you still need grains." In this case, it was the Indian reporter who was other-worldly and Śrīla Prabhupāda who pointed out that Kṛṣṇa consciousness is not meant for armchair speculation but for solving basic problems like hunger.

Śrīla Prabhupāda referred to the same verse, *annād bhavanti bhūtāni,* a few months later when meeting with the governor of Geneva, Switzerland. The governor had asked, "If everyone becomes Kṛṣṇa conscious, won't the economy be in trouble?" Prabhupāda said, "No," and then quoted the verse *annād bhavanti bhūtāni.* "Everyone subsists on food grains," said Śrīla Prabhupāda, and he proposed that if everyone cultivated his own land and kept cows, there would be no economic problem. People should live simply and spend their saved time solving the problems of birth, death, old age, and disease. After that meeting with the governor of Geneva, Prabhupāda asked, "Were my answers all right?" I replied that the governor had asked about the economy because he thought that the devotees were simply beggars. "Therefore," Prabhupāda said, "I talked about tilling the land. We are not beggars. We are giving the highest knowledge. Besides, we gave him a book of highest knowledge, *Bhagavad-gītā,* but he could not give us anything." Through all his acts and words, Śrīla Prabhupāda remained transcendental, and yet in a down-to-earth and logical way he confronted whomever he met with the necessity of implementing Kṛṣṇa consciousness. Upon meeting a policeman, he asked him to implement Kṛṣṇa consciousness in his work, and he also advised a college president, a commercial airlines pilot, and a fine artist in a similar way.

Gradually, I am beginning to understand that Śrīla Prabhupāda's request to me that we demonstrate how to solve all problems by Kṛṣṇa consciousness is something that has to be carried on in many ways by many people. For example, the Kṛṣṇa conscious farm communities are meant for demonstrating the efficacy of cow protection as a practical way of life. If a man has cows which supply him milk, and if he has grains which supply him basic food, and if he learns to live in self-sufficiency without depending on amenities like gasoline and tractors, then he will be successful even if there is war or an economic collapse. Thus the *varṇāśrama* demonstration of farm communities is an important dimension of Śrīla Prabhupāda's mission to demonstrate how to solve problems with Kṛṣṇa consciousness.

Prabhupāda also wanted us to demonstrate Kṛṣṇa consciousness by practically developing broad strategies for recruiting devotees in countries throughout the world. Wonderfully fulfilling this order, Śrīla Prabhupāda's disciples like Bhagavān Goswami have been "writing" many volumes of eloquent proof that the Kṛṣṇa consciousness movement can solve people's problems.

In the area of education, the Kṛṣṇa consciousness movement is still in a pioneer stage after less than twenty years since its inception. But the ISKCON leaders are now aware that the next generation of devotees has to be educated in the spirit and philosophy of Kṛṣṇa consciousness, while at the same time individuals' psychophysical tendencies must be guided in terms of the Vedic divisions for *daivi-varṇāśrama*. Although a pure Vaiṣṇava is always above all caste divisions, different devotees will want to work in different ways, and they should be well prepared.

Śrīla Prabhupāda's request to successfully demonstrate Kṛṣṇa consciousness also includes programs to approach and cultivate people who may not ultimately want to live in the *āśrama* communities of ISKCON. People who are already engaged in occupational work in the different divisions of *varṇāśrama* should learn how to dovetail their skills in the service of Kṛṣṇa. This is described by Nārada Muni in the First Canto of *Śrīmad-Bhāgavatam:*

> O *brāhmaṇa* Vyāsadeva, it is decided by the learned that the best remedial measure for removing all troubles and miseries is to dedicate one's activities to the service of the Supreme Lord Personality of Godhead [Śrī Kṛṣṇa]."
>
> (*Bhāg*. 1.5.32)

In the purport to this verse Śrīla Prabhupāda comments that "it does not matter what one is. If one is an administrator, statesman, warrior, politician, etc., then one should try to establish the Lord's supremacy in statesmanship . . . If one is a businessman, an industrialist, an agriculturalist, etc., then one should spend his hard-earned money for the cause of the Lord."

But only if the Kṛṣṇa consciousness movement continues to develop a core of hardworking, pure devotees will it be able to "write the book" which Prabhupāda has requested of us. We have to show how to solve problems by actually solving them in ISKCON and by sharing our solutions with the world. We have to show "why things fail without Kṛṣṇa" by ourselves *not* failing and by ourselves never being without Kṛṣṇa. And this work is to be carried out by every Kṛṣṇa conscious devotee, not only by a few leaders or a few writers.

As for my writing a book, as Prabhupāda requested, that I may also do one day, and I do not wish to shun this duty. But I think it is more important for me to understand that Prabhupāda is requesting me to work along with all his followers to help bring about the spiritual revolution predicted by Lord Caitanya. When we think of what it actually means to influence world politics and mass society and world culture, we may ask, "How is this all possible?" For an affirmative answer we may remember that if one is empowered by Kṛṣṇa and *guru* then everything is possible. "By the grace of the spiritual master, a lame man can cross mountains, a blind man can see the stars in the sky, and a dumb man can speak like a great orator."

mūkaṁ karoti vācālaṁ
paṅguṁ laṅghayate girim
yat kṛpā tam aham vande
śrī guruṁ dīna-tāriṇam

Literary contributions also play a part, but this is not the job of one or two devotees; it should be taken up combinedly. Śrīla Prabhupāda desired that his disciples read his books, assimilate the subject matter, and express their realizations by writing articles for *Back to Godhead*. The literary problems of presenting Kṛṣṇa consciousness in a way that is neither dogmatic nor naive, and yet is not too entangling in speculative research or name-calling, are problems to be solved by experience as well as by realization in Kṛṣṇa consciousness. And all these can be worked out by sharing exchanges among the devotees.

When the devotees regularly produce excellent books and magazine articles, and as they continue to distribute Prabhupāda's books more and more, and when they establish successful farm communities, and when they solve their own problems of education, marriage, and community cooperation, and when they demonstrate the perfect Vaiṣṇava etiquette of ladies and gentlemen—not just with a handful of members, but with thousands—then eventually the dull brains of the suffering population of Kali-yuga will come to realize Prabhupāda's message, and we can be satisfied by fulfilling his request. If there is truth in the homely proverb "Build a better mousetrap and the world will beat a path to your door," then it should not be very long before the practical ability of devotees to solve their problems and the problems of other people in the world begins to manifest more clearly to everyone, and the world's citizens begin a mass movement of beating their path to the Kṛṣṇa consciousness movement and back to Godhead.

The *Īśopaniṣad* verse *asuryā nāma te lokāḥ* describes the fate of the *asuras* if this transformation of the world through

Kṛṣṇa consciousness does not take place. Śrīla Prabhupāda once wrote that demoniac leaders comprise five percent of the world's population, yet they are misleading the remaining ninety-five percent, who are ignorant yet innocent. He said it is the mission of Kṛṣṇa consciousness to save both the five percent and the ninety-five percent. Now almost one hundred percent of the people are living as killers of the soul, both by killing animals as well as their own selves and their children through materialistic education, which neglects self-realization. As Prabhupāda points out in his purport to this verse, these *asuras* and their followers reject Kṛṣṇa consciousness, thinking that it is not going to help their economic development. But even after putting aside the best part of life, the *asuras* still are not able to solve their economic problems. This is because things undertaken without Kṛṣṇa fail. The foolish *asuras* lose out, therefore, both materially and spiritually.

This is also described by Prahlāda Mahārāja in his instructions to his demoniac schoolmates. Of Prahlāda's teachings, Prabhupāda writes the following:

> We see materialistic persons busily engaged in economic development all day and night, trying to increase their material opulence, but even if we suppose that they get some benefit from such endeavors, that does not solve the problems of their lives. Nor do they know what the real problem of life is.
>
> (*Bhāg* 7.6.4)

Those in the line of disciplic succession from Prahlāda Mahārāja and from Śrīla Prabhupāda are the real benefactors of humankind. It is their duty to remain compassionate toward the sons and daughters of the demons and to show them the ways and means of Kṛṣṇa consciousness. This is the gist of Śrīla Prabhupāda's request.

XV
Śrīla Prabhupāda Praṇati

nama oṁ viṣṇu pādāya kṛṣṇa-preṣṭhāya bhū-tale
śrīmate bhaktivedānta-svāmin iti nāmine

namas te sārasvate deve gaura-vāṇī pracāriṇe
nirviśeṣa-śūnyavādi-pāścātya deśa-tāriṇe

"I offer my respectful obeisances unto His Divine Grace A. C. Bhaktivedanta Swami Prabhupāda, who is very dear to Lord Kṛṣṇa, having taken shelter at His lotus feet.

"Our respectful obeisances are unto you, O spiritual master, servant of Sarasvatī Gosvāmī. You are kindly preaching the message of Lord Caitanyadeva and are delivering the Western countries, which are filled with impersonalism and voidism."

The first time I *heard* the Prabhupāda *praṇāma-mantra* was when Śrīla Prabhupāda ordered me to repeat it word for word after him at the time of my initiation in September 1966. He had just chanted the first round on my red wooden *japa* beads while I reverently watched. Then he called me up beside him. He handed back the beads and said, "Bow down." Then he said, "Repeat after me. *Namaḥ*." I repeated, "*Namaḥ*." And word by word we proceeded until I had recited the whole prayer. *Nama oṁ viṣṇu pādāya kṛṣṇa-preṣṭhāya bhū-tale/ śrīmate bhaktivedānta-svāmin iti nāmine.* As I recited the Sanskrit, my eyes were closed and I felt myself plunging into a state of devotion and surrender. I experienced intense feelings that I was entering eternal life. And then Śrīla Prabhupāda gave me my spiritual name.

The first time I *saw* the *mantra* written out was a few days after my initiation. Śrīla Prabhupāda had given his evening lecture, and we had just finished a half hour of rousing *kīrtana*. That evening, a college friend of mine was attending our storefront for the first (and last) time, and I was preoccupied with trying to make him feel at ease. One of the devotees came up to us and handed me a piece of carbon copy paper on which was printed a list of Prabhupāda's disciples from the two initiations he had held—about fifteen names. At the bottom of the page was the mantra *nama oṁ* . . . and an English translation. I was excited to see it but folded it and placed it in my pocket to look at after my skeptical friend had departed. Later, when I reached my apartment, I took out the paper and read it to myself.

nama oṁ viṣṇu pādāya kṛṣṇa-preṣṭhāya bhū-tale
śrīmate bhaktivedānta-svāmin iti nāmine

> I offer my respectful obeisances unto His Divine Grace A. C. Bhaktivedanta Swami Prabhupāda, who is very dear to Lord Kṛṣṇa on this earth, having taken shelter at the lotus feet of the transcendental Lord.

The word *obeisances* never meant anything to me before I met Śrīla Prabhupāda, but now it was a surcharged, sacred reality. I offered my obeisances to His Divine Grace again and again. Prabhupāda's translation, "A. C. Bhaktivedanta Swami, who is very dear to Lord Kṛṣṇa on this earth," really struck me. It described the intimate relationship between Lord Kṛṣṇa and Śrīla Prabhupāda. As far as we were concerned, *no one* was more dear "on this earth" to Lord Kṛṣṇa than Śrīla Prabhupāda, who was single handedly spreading Kṛṣṇa consciousness worldwide. Certainly, to we followers on the Lower East Side there was only *māyā* and Swamiji. The new *mantra* would help us express our appreciation.

Now, along with speaking the *mantra* out loud, we were also bowing down to Prabhupāda and offering *daṇḍavats*. Whenever we saw Śrīla Prabhupāda, we would say the *mantra* and bow down before him. We did it, for example, when several of us reported to him up in his room after shaving our heads for the first time. And we bowed down whenever we saw him coming into the temple room, especially at the beginning of an evening program, and then after the *kīrtana* and again after the lecture. This was a way of thanking Prabhupāda and very deliberately surrendering and offering him the respects one should offer to the representative of God. In fact, some boys lost their enthusiasm and stopped coming because they said they were turned off once the bowing and praying to Swamiji started. But for us who became Śrīla Prabhupāda's disciples, there was no problem in bowing down; we did it with great pride and joy at having such a rare and qualified spiritual master.

Very few other overt ways of showing respect to our spiritual master were as dramatic as the recitation of the prayer and the offering of *daṇḍavats*. Years later, Śrīla Prabhupāda remarked in lectures, "These boys are so nice that even if they see me a hundred times, then a hundred times they bow down." He took it as a sign of a devotee's good etiquette as a Vaiṣṇava. As described in a *Śrīmad-Bhāgavatam* narration, Mahārāja Parīkṣit humbly offered his respect to the saints and *rājarṣis* who had gathered to see him: "The Emperor received them properly and bowed his head to the ground." (*Bhāg* 1.19.11) In his commentary on this verse Śrīla Prabhupāda writes, "The system of bowing the head to the ground to show respect to superiors is an excellent etiquette which obliges the honored guest deep into the heart. Even the first-grade offender is excused simply by this process."

The bowing down continued to be an issue, however, with guests and envious onlookers. Once, in a question-

and-answer period after a lecture, a guest told Prabhupāda that he didn't feel subordinate to anyone, and therefore he didn't feel he had to bow down to anyone. He seemed to be indirectly criticizing the devotees' offering of obeisances to Prabhupāda. Prabhupāda replied, "That is your material disease . . . to think that you don't have to bow down." Śrīla Prabhupāda then demonstrated logically that nature forces each of us to be subordinate, to "bow down" to old age, disease, death, and many other things. Since we are being forced to bow down, we should find out where we will be happy by bowing down. "And that is Kṛṣṇa," said Prabhupāda. "Your bowing down will not be stopped, because you were meant for that; but if you bow down to Kṛṣṇa and Kṛṣṇa's representative, then you become happy."

There were many new occasions on which we now used the *mantra* to Śrīla Prabhupāda. Śrīla Prabhupāda encouraged the devotees to greet each other in the morning by making obeisances and by addressing each other regularly as *prabhu,* or master. Whenever the *prabhus* offered each other obeisances, they always accompanied it by reciting the *mantra* in praise of Śrīla Prabhupāda. We heard that there were other Vaiṣṇava *mantras,* yet to pray to our spiritual father seemed fitting and best. The Prabhupāda *mantra* helped establish our family of devotees, especially when sometimes there was a quarrel between devotees. Prabhupāda said that the offending devotees should offer obeisances to each other, and at that time also they recited the *praṇāma-mantra*—for bringing devotees together under Prabhupāda.

Offering obeisances to Śrīla Prabhupāda by singing his *mantra* in *kīrtana* was the most assuring experience. If the Pañca-Tattva *mantra,* the prayers to Lord Caitanya and His associates, is more lenient than the Hare Kṛṣṇa *mantra* and is therefore always chanted at the beginning of a *kīrtana,* then the Prabhupāda *praṇati* can be considered an even further extension of Kṛṣṇa's mercy. We especially felt it when we went out to chant in public. Usually as soon as we devotees arrived people gathered around at the sight of our odd dress and appearance. We would pick up our instruments, wrap the *karatāla* cords around our fingers, test the *mṛdaṅga* drum, line up, start the rhythm, shift our feet—and then the first singing words that we uttered were *nama oṁ viṣṇu pādāya kṛṣṇa-preṣṭhāya bhū-tale/ śrīmate bhaktivedānta-svāmin iti nāmine*. When opening a *kīrtana* with this *mantra* in a public place, I have always thought how the people cannot possibly know what we are singing. They are more familiar with the Hare Kṛṣṇa *mantra*. But chanting the Prabhupāda *praṇati* is more for the devotees; it is our opening prayer to Prabhupāda, and it gives us courage to go on with the *kīrtana*. As one *harināma* devotee remarked, "Unless we chant the *mantra* to Prabhupāda, the other *mantras* won't work."

Halls, schools, and homes offered a more controlled environment for singing *kīrtana*, and audiences usually showed some respect and interest. It was the taste of bliss to chant *bhaktivedānta-svāmin iti nāmine* and to celebrate our identity before others, as *śīṣyas* of Śrīla Prabhupāda. We were not followers of any other *guru*, nor were we pretenders claiming we didn't need a *guru*—we were surrendered to Prabhupāda, and singing it.

When the devotees in London made their hit recording of the Hare Kṛṣṇa *mantra* with Apple Records, the flip side was the *mantra* to Śrīla Prabhupāda. The Hare Kṛṣṇa *mantra* became very popular, rising on the charts to become number one in Czechoslovakia and West Germany, number four in Australia, and in the top ten in England. That meant that thousands of people were also regularly hearing and enjoying praises to Prabhupāda in music. We had a copy of the record in Boston, and we played it often in the large, empty rooms of the building we had recently purchased. Soon after we moved in, local hoodlums had attacked us, broken many windows, and thrown firebombs. Although they were arrested, they threatened to come back again, and for weeks our temple family lived in an alert state of anxiety. During those long autumn weeks, we stayed together and went on hearing the London recording of the Prabhupāda *praṇati* until the song became like our theme, somehow expressing our vulnerability and yet our protection at the lotus feet of Śrīla Prabhupāda.

Once introduced, the Prabhupāda *praṇati* was used as a prayer for offering food to Kṛṣṇa. There were other prayers as well, but Śrīla Prabhupāda affirmed that the prayers to the spiritual master were sufficient.

> For offering prasadam, present everything before the spiritual master whose picture is also on the altar, that means that the spiritual master will take care of offering the foodstuff to the Lord. Therefore simply by chanting the prayer to the spiritual master, everything will be complete.
>
> (Letter of May 1, 1968)

The *praṇāma-mantra* of Śrīla Prabhupāda was humbly recited by his followers in every conceivable instance, such as when a disciple was introduced to another swami, or in the occasion of bowing down in any church or place of worship, and sometimes before parents and other startled relatives and friends. When Deity worship began in the temples, devotees bowed down before the Supreme Lord and recited the one *mantra* they were most sure of, *nama oṁ viṣṇu-pādāya kṛṣṇa-preṣṭhāya bhū-tale/ śrīmate bhaktivedānta-svāmin iti nāmine*.

After three years, Śrīla Prabhupāda composed and gave his disciples a second *mantra*, *namas te sārasvate deve gaura-vāṇī pracāriṇe/ nirviśeṣa-śūnyavādi-pāścātya deśa-tāriṇe*. I was in Boston when we received our copy in the mail. Bharadrāja dāsa, a musically talented devotee, quickly made a nice tune for the *mantra*, which is still sung by devotees today. A devotee in California wrote to Śrīla Prabhupāda thanking him for the second *mantra* and commenting how we were such dependent neophytes that Śrīla Prabhupāda had to himself supply us with prayers to our spiritual master. We were all very interested in the meaning of the new *mantra*. Out of all possible descriptions of his mission, Śrīla Prabhupāda had chosen to state it as "delivering the Western countries, which are filled with impersonalism and voidism." Prabhupāda's mission was our mission—to assist him in preaching the message of Lord Caitanya by attacking the forces of *nirviśeṣa* and *śūnyavādi*. The two *mantras* taken together are themselves a formidable utterance against impersonalism.

The philosophical content of the Prabhupāda *praṇati* is not unlike other verses describing the *guru*-disciple relationship, such as Arjuna's initial surrender to Kṛṣṇa (*Bhagavad-gītā* 2.7) or verses like *tad vijñānārthaṁ sa gurum evābhigacchet* and *tad viddhi praṇipātena paripraśnena sevayā*. Although many sastric verses recommend surrender to "the *guru*," the Prabhupāda *praṇati* is more specific and personal: it is the surrender to and praise of Śrīla Prabhupāda by his own loving disciples. The *mantras* have a homemade, family feeling, and yet they are correctly composed in Sanskrit and exactly in accord with *paramparā*.

The Vaiṣṇava's *praṇati* differ from that of the impersonalists in another way also. The Vaiṣṇava considers himself the eternal servant of his spiritual master; he does not serve the spiritual master for a certain duration, in a time-serving mood, and then later "become one with Brahman" and thus no longer think himself servant of his *guru*. Therefore the Prabhupāda *praṇati* is in the Vaiṣṇava tradition of staunch personalism. Whereas the impersonalists all worship their *guru* on a special "*guru pūrṇimā* day," the Vaiṣṇava disciples prefer to offer the special worship of the year to their spiritual master on his own personal birthday. Although the Prabhupāda *praṇati mantras* were introduced in a humble, informal way by Śrīla Prabhupāda, they are highly significant for his followers. They are a disciple's meditation as the eternal servant of Śrīla Prabhupāda.

Furthermore, by worshiping Śrīla Prabhupāda, his follower worships and serves all the spiritual masters in disciplic succession. Śrīla Prabhupāda explained this in a letter:

> Regarding your question: "Is it not true that by service I am with you?" It is very correct. You are not only in connection with me, but you are connected with the whole parampara, up to Krsna. It is so nice a thing. By service only we are connected.
>
> (Letter of 1968)

Chanting the Prabhupāda *praṇati* makes us conscious of the honor, worship, and surrender we owe to Śrīla Prabhupāda. When uttered sincerely and not in mechanical forgetfulness, the *mantras* act to bind us close to Prabhupāda's lotus feet. As it is stated, he is Bhaktivedanta Swami by name, and he has come to deliver us from nescience and to set us on the path back to Godhead. We chant the holy name of Kṛṣṇa under his guidance, and we hear all the Vedic *śāstras* from him. By his grace, he has rescued us from a horrible condition of material life, and so we offer him our respectful obeisances.

The disciples' obeisances as expressed in the Prabhupāda *praṇati* are an act of humility. Bowing down to a living person whenever you meet him and uttering a prayer of obeisances to him cannot be performed by one who is proud. Neither should such honor be offered to an ordinary person. It is offered by a humble servant of the servant to a true Vaiṣṇava. In the case of Śrīla Prabhupāda, there is no doubt that he is a Vaiṣṇava spiritual master, a genuine, transparent via medium to Kṛṣṇa, and so the disciple's humility, as expressed in offering *daṇḍavats* and the Prabhupāda *praṇati*, is very well placed and for the disciple's greatest benefit.

The purifying effect of humbly approaching great souls is recommended throughout the Vedic literature. Lord Caitanya set the example Himself by praising the qualities of Sanātana Gosvāmī.

> By seeing you, by touching you, and by glorifying your transcendental qualities, one can perfect the purpose of all sense activity. This is the verdict of the revealed scriptures.
>
> My dear Vaiṣṇava, seeing a person like you is the perfection of one's eyesight. Touching your lotus feet is the perfection of the sense of touch. Glorifying your good qualities is the tongue's real activity, for in the material world it is very difficult to find a pure devotee of the Lord.

The spiritual master is the representative of God, and therefore he should be respected as being as good as God, just as the viceroy of the king is due all the respects owed to the king. Honestly thinking of himself always as a fool before his spiritual master, a sincere disciple recites his *guru's praṇāma-mantra,* inquires humbly from him about transcendental knowledge, and enthusiastically renders service as a menial servant.

Although we have stressed that it takes humility to chant the Prabhupāda *praṇati,* the *mantras* are actually a possession more valuable than the rarest jewel and the source of greatest satisfaction for the devotee who can utter them in factual submission to Śrīla Prabhupāda.

The first of the two *mantras* is a standard verse used even before Śrīla Prabhupāda's appearance by disciples of previous spiritual masters. And after Śrīla Prabhupāda's disappearance, the same basic *mantra* is used by disciples of the present spiritual masters in ISKCON. By inserting the name of one bona fide *guru* or another, the same *mantra* is used in *paramparā*. And yet both these specific *mantras* known as Prabhupāda *praṇati* will always be sung and uttered, even though many generations of spiritual masters will appear after Śrīla Prabhupāda. Just as Śrīla Prabhupāda's *mūrti* is placed in the ISKCON temples and will continue to be placed in the center of worship in future generations, so his *praṇāma-mantras* will always be sung.

Although we have referred to these *mantras* as "home-made," they will continue to be recited just like classical Vedic *ślokas,* and His Divine Grace A.C. Bhaktivedanta Swami Prabhupāda will never be forgotten. Śrīla Prabhupāda is the fountainhead, founder-*ācārya* of ISKCON, and all future devotees in the Kṛṣṇa consciousness movement continue to be part of his expanding family. We will continue always to feel the pride and joy, and the safety, of our identity as Prabhupāda's *śiṣyas,* as expressed by the Prabhupāda *mantras.*

Our assertions regarding the special place of Prabhupāda and his *praṇama-mantras* are not sentimental claims. Lord Kṛṣṇa chose Śrīla Prabhupāda to be the founder-*ācārya* of the Kṛṣṇa consciousness movement in the modern age. Those people of the Western world who actually desire spiritual life should run after their connection to Śrīla Prabhupāda in disciplic succession, just as Bhaktivinoda Ṭhākura sings, "Kṛṣṇa is yours; you have the power to give Him to me. I am simply running behind you, shouting, 'Kṛṣṇa! Kṛṣṇa!' "

I sometimes think of Śrīla Prabhupāda and his disciples in relation to the story of Lord Brahmā when he went to call upon Lord Kṛṣṇa in Dvārakā. When Lord Brahmā was met at the door by Kṛṣṇa's doorkeeper, who asked for his name, at first Lord Brahmā said, "Tell Lord Kṛṣṇa that Lord Brahmā has come." But Lord Brahmā was soon surprised to hear that Kṛṣṇa had asked, "Which Lord Brahmā has come?" Although he was humiliated, Lord Brahmā retained his good sense and asked the doorman to introduce him as the father of the four Kumāras. When these credentials were presented to Lord Kṛṣṇa, the Lord agreed to see Lord Brahmā, even though he is one of millions of different Brahmās in the material creation, and in fact the smallest of all Brahmās. In telling of this transcendental incident, Śrīla Prabhupāda pointed out that Lord Brahmā was recognized by Kṛṣṇa when he gave his name in relationship to recognized devotees, the four Kumāras. So when I sometimes wonder how it is possible for Lord Kṛṣṇa to see any good in my activities or to even recognize who I am, I reflect that my only credit is my connection to Śrīla Prabhupāda. Our discredits may be many, and our spiritual significance may be nil, but if we can factually state that we are related to the great Vaiṣṇava His Divine Grace A.C. Bhaktivedanta Swami Prabhupāda, surely Kṛṣṇa will recognize us as one of the eternal associates of Lord Caitanya. And we shall be known by this *mantra:*

nama oṁ viṣṇu-pādāya kṛṣṇa-preṣṭhāya bhū-tale
śrīmate bhaktivedānta-svāmin iti nāmine

namas te sārasvate deve gaura-vānī pracāriṇe
nirviśeṣa-śūnyavādi-pāścātya désa-tāriṇe

ACKNOWLEDGMENTS

Editing — Dattatreya dāsa
Design — Yamarāja dāsa
Production — Gaura-pūrṇimā dāsa
Typesetting — Gaura-pūrṇimā dāsa
Chandramukhi-devī dāsī
Paste-up — Sādhana-siddhi dāsa
Antima dāsa
Gaura-pūrṇimā dāsa
Graphics — Antima dāsa
Sanskrit Editing — Agrahya dāsa